From PERSIA *to*
TEHR ANGELES

From PERSIA to TEHR ANGELES

*A Contemporary Guide
to Understanding and
Appreciating Ancient
Persian Culture*

KAMRAN SHARAREH
Chef KShar

NEW YORK

From PERSIA to TEHR ANGELES
A Contemporary Guide to Understanding
and Appreciating Ancient Persian Culture

ISBN 978-1-61448-577-3 paperback
ISBN 978-1-61448-578-0 eBook
ISBN 978-1-61448-579-7 audio
Library of Congress Control Number: 2013941185

Morgan James Publishing
The Entrepreneurial Publisher
5 Penn Plaza, 23rd Floor,
New York City, New York 10001
(212) 655-5470 office • (516) 908-4496 fax
www.MorganJamesPublishing.com

Cover Design by:
Rachel Lopez
www.r2cdesign.com

Interior Design by:
Bonnie Bushman
bonnie@caboodlegraphics.com

In an effort to support local communities, raise awareness and funds, Morgan James Publishing donates a percentage of all book sales for the life of each book to Habitat for Humanity Peninsula and Greater Williamsburg.

Get involved today, visit
www.MorganJamesBuilds.com.

I would like to dedicate this book to the **new generation** of Iranian-Americans—especially my two wonderful children, my daughter Niyaz and my son Alireza—for guiding me onto the path of the heart of their generation.

This book also is dedicated to the **older generation**, especially my dear mother and departed father, for teaching me what they knew best and allowing me to leave the nest to grow.

And last but not least, with this book I honor **my own generation**—especially my dear wife Nazaneen, as well as others—for holding one another gently enough so as not to be crushed by the changes and pressures from both sides, the other two generations.

Contents

ACKNOWLEDGMENTS

In life we get to meet a lot of people, but only a very few will impact our lives in a truly positive way. A few years ago, I was very fortunate to meet Mr. Jamak Golshani, whom today I am honored to call my dear friend. I want to thank him for having faith in me and trusting me enough to push me to capture my dream. It's because of the selflessness, generosity, time, and effort that he put into making me stand for what I believe in, and into pushing me past my limits by coaching me, that I can stand tall and be proud of who I am today.

I would also like to thank another dear friend, Mr. Mohsen Shah, for his true support and understanding throughout my life—for giving me a leg to stand on and a shoulder to lean against in my times of need.

My dear reader, may you get to be as lucky as I have been when it comes to friendship. Love your friends and hold them near your heart. They are the ones who will help you rise to your best potential.

TO MY DEAR READERS

Welcome to the world of *From Persia to Tehrangeles*.

Before you even read the book, I want to thank you for picking it up. For in doing this, you give me the opportunity to share with you the love in my heart, by giving you part of me.

And because *you* are who I wrote the book for, I also want to thank you for the beautiful journey I have gotten to take by writing it. In exploring through writing such an essential aspect of my life as the journey from the old country (the "Persia" of the book's title) to the ways of the new country ("Tehrangeles"), in order to inform, inspire, counsel, and strengthen you, I have grown so much, myself. I am not the same person as when I first started writing the book. And on a broader level, what I have been called to write about has greatly increased my respect for humankind and the problems each one of us goes through in life.

So I hope that in reading this book you will not only be able to benefit from my growth, but also get to experience your own beneficial growth, and find yourself opening doors that you never imagined existed.

You will love the journey you are about to embark on, here. Of that, I feel confident. For not only will you get to know the Persian ways (in the old and new countries) as well as me and my journey, but you also will learn more about who *you* are and where you want to be in life.

So consider this book as a gift of guidance. You are about to begin this journey, and I am here at the finish line, passionately waiting for you to arrive so that we can start the next phase of our journey together. You could think of me as a male midwife, in this regard: waiting to catch you, embrace you, and welcome you to your new world—whether you are:

- An Iranian immigrant from the older generation;
- Iranian-American;
- Marrying into an Iranian-American family;
- Or simply wanting to learn more about Iranians, the old Persian culture, and the modern world of "Tehrangeles."

Please take your time in reading. The book is meant to inform you, delight you, perhaps occasionally sadden you, and overall, to support you in becoming whole.

I wish you a wonderful journey. I will be waiting for you on the other side.

—Kamran Sharareh
Pleasanton, California, USA

INTRODUCTION

I come from a country with ancient roots and woven carpets. A country where you could walk through the *bazar* and smell attar of roses. Where you could knock on the door of almost any anyone's home and walk inside without prior notice, and be welcomed with cups of tea fresh from the samovar, sweets, and smiles.

In the country I come from, the New Year takes place in mid-March. And for over a month beforehand and a few weeks afterwards, it was celebrated with rituals such as: housecleaning (literal and symbolic); special cooking; burning dried weed to make a fire after sunset, and jumping over the fire (with young children in arms) to ensure good health in the coming year ("Take my yellowness, and give me your redness," the saying translates to—*Zardi-man-az-to, sorkhi-to-az-man*); giving away money; visiting one's extended family, starting with the elders; on the 13th day after the new year, picnicking outdoors to avert misfortune; and many more customs based on secular and religious premises.

In the country I come from, marriages were arranged, and the process of choosing a bride was elaborate. By the time the wedding reception took place (which could be up to a year after the wedding ceremony, during which interval the husband and wife still would not have cohabited), all sorts of specific arrangements had been done and traditions enacted in order for the bride and groom to begin living their lives together. And it was a given that they were not only marrying each other: they were marrying the extended family as well—a whole community.

Community was so much part of the old world that the whole modern concept of individual freedoms did not so much enter into that life. In the more public of the public bath houses, for example (especially in the days before indoor plumbing), men and women would each go to a separate bath house, there to drape themselves in a cloth and share the waters with their neighbors. (In the other kind of bath house, you could rent a room for yourself and your immediate family.)

In the country I come from, for some people religion is not separate from daily life but underlies it. At times of major life passages, such as death, each of the intricate rituals that plays its part in the burial ceremony—from the prayers, to the shrouding of the body, to the positioning of the body, and so on—has a very profound spiritual corollary meant to serve the soul of the departed, as well as that person's surviving relatives. Religion also undergirds much of the New Year's preparations and celebrations, how animals are killed for meat, and of course marriage and birth.

In the country I come from, food was abundant and richly important, and played a stabilizing role in family life. Each day three meals were cooked, all of which the family ate together at home. Foods were bought daily, before the advent of freezers, and the shops would provide fresh-baked breads, meats, produce, herbs, and whatever else was needed. Recipes ranged from simple to lavish, depending on the occasion and the family's financial situation. Cooking could take half a day, depending; and special occasions, like New Year's, weddings, family gatherings after someone had died, and so on required special foods that often turned into feasts.

Beauty showed itself, in the country I come from, almost everywhere: in the buildings, with their intricate mosaics and wood-carved ornamentations; in the carpets on the floor, woven according to ways and patterns set down centuries before; in the music, often soulful tunes played on flutes and stringed instruments, and sometimes sung by a singer who might improvise; in the poetry, some of which is still torrentially popular in the modern world of my country, and even *this* country—not only the

"Epic of Kings" from centuries ago, the *Shahnameh*, but also the mystical love poetry of the mystics Omar Khayyam, Rumi (said to be the best-selling poet of our time), and Hafiz. Beauty showed itself in the language, in how people addressed each other as a matter of course ("My dear…").

I come from a beautiful tradition; a country with so much worth preserving.

And yet I left that country. I left it to come to America. I wanted the freedoms I had found here when I'd first come visiting as a student. By now, I have lived here about four decades, long enough to have experienced the journey of what it is like to live between two cultures, to try to adapt to the new one while still keeping the best of the old.

This journey is not only mine: about 1.5 million Iranians have left Iran for the United States, and other countries as well. So others have gone, or will go through, what I went through. I want to make use of the wisdom of my experience to make the way easier for those people to come, and to make the way easier for those who have already arrived but who may not know that much about the country of their parents and grandparents.

I spent the early part of my life, here, learning to adapt to the new ways, in the process appreciating the best of what they had to offer. So I understand something about what needs to be adapted to, and how to go about doing it. This book will be your "guidebook" through the old ways and the new ways. You may be from the generation who moved here directly from Iran. Or you may be a child of an Iranian immigrant from the older generation, perhaps now with children of your own. Perhaps you are not Iranian, but are marrying into the world of an Iranian-American and want to understand your spouse's culture. Or maybe you simply want to have a better, closer understanding of Iran and its people in the United States and other countries—an understanding not distorted by media fears and prejudices, but gleaned directly from one who knows the territory first-hand. Whatever your situation, my hope is that you will come to appreciate the best of the old ways (not all of which should be carried forth! For example, not being able to choose your own spouse), if they have not been familiar to you; and that, for the older generation, you will come to appreciate the modern ways of the younger generation in this country.

Good communication depends on understanding. Too often, people whose lives take place in different countries from their parents or children, with greatly different experiences, don't understand enough about each other's situation to have good communication. But to me, the past is where I came from, and the future is where I am going: my parents represent the past, but my children represent the future. And so I have made it my business to appreciate my children's ways that they learned from the country I myself brought them to, and to give my children space, respect, honor, and to learn from them.

So I welcome you to come with me on this journey through old Iran, and the new world of Iranians in America—what they call "Tehrangeles" (because of the 700,000-800,000 Iranian-Americans living in Los Angeles). Along the way, I will point out some of the challenges of adapting to the new world, as well as telling you about the old ways that even the children of Iranian immigrants to America may not know much about. And I will share myself with you enroute, so that you may know something of my story, who it is who is opening these windows for you, and invite you to see through my eyes what is important in life; what makes for true happiness.

There is a wealth of discovery to be made here. There is a wealth of richness and beauty and customs from ancient times in Persia that are worth knowing. There is a wealth of new innovation and freedoms that the younger generation of Iranian-Americans have broken ground—for their own sakes, and maybe for ours, too. And there is a wealth of wisdom possible in your own heart and being, which I hope—as you read this book—will make itself more and more and more known to you.

Chapter 1

FROM PERSIA TO TEHRANGELES

Three Generations in the New World

COMING TO THE U.S. TO LEARN FROM
THE NEW WORLD, THEN TAKE IT BACK HOME

When I left the richness of my homeland—an ancient land called Persia, in the old days, and called Iran, today—I was only seventeen, and I had no thought of leaving it permanently. As an Iranian, I was steeped in the ancient ways of my country and culture. Some had been passed down to me over generations, with specific instructions, rules, and admonitions; but most of them simply accrued to me as someone who lived there, as part of the atmosphere I breathed. Daily family meals, prayers five times a day, dishes made redolent with rosewater and saffron, the *ghazals* of ancient poets still ringing in my ears—one did not have to go far to experience the great wealth of culture that made its way into daily life.

Yet I also was impressed, like many others of my generation, by much of what the West had to offer—its drive, its modernity, its fast track to success, and more—and I wanted to avail myself of its benefits, both for myself and for those back in my country. So, trembling with nervousness as much as excitement (it was my first time leaving the family nest, and a very difficult transition), I packed up my things and went to the United States to study business at a university in California.

I had to start from the beginning as a visitor to the U.S., learning a brand-new language and adjusting to a new culture. But I enjoyed my life here as a student. I made friends, among them some other Persians; I married and had a family; and I found some of the American ways I encountered quite freeing, especially the assumption that one could direct one's own life, instead of living according to one's parents' wishes, only.

My plan was to stay long enough to get a degree, and then to bring the fruits of what I had learned back to the country of my birth—which had given so much to me—and resume living there. My plan was to view my time in America as simply an interval in the ongoing story of my life in Iran.

Yet you know what they say: "If you want to make God laugh, make plans." My plans did not turn out exactly as I intended. After I had obtained three degrees—a BA in business and marketing, a BS in business education, followed by a Masters in business administration, it seemed the time to return to Iran to make a difference.

But my wife (who was also Persian) knew me better than I knew myself.

"Let us stay here. You will be happier here," she told me.

"What do you mean?" I asked her. "Iran is my country, my people. I want to give back. I owe them. My country needs educated people like myself."

And so we packed our bags and moved—my wife, our young daughter, and me—to Iran.

THE OLD COUNTRY ISN'T WHAT IT USED TO BE ONCE YOU'VE TASTED FREEDOM

Once back in Iran, I was fortunate to get a good-paying job right away. I worked for the only car-manufacturing company. My job was to set up their marketing department. It took me one year to do that; then I was promoted to Vice President of Sales, where I expected to apply my business and marketing knowledge to improving the sales department. But in Iran at that time, it didn't matter what your job title was: you were asked to do things that had nothing to do with your job. So that was frustrating. And just as frustrating, they even tried to control me when I was off work—such as dictating what I could wear in public.

And the challenges I had to face in my own country went on from there.

For example, my family needed housing. I either had to rent or to buy a place. But in Iran, you have to buy everything in cash, and I did not have enough cash to buy a house. Furthermore, no bank would lend me money to buy a house. Having left at only seventeen, I had no credit and no credit background. I could have gotten by on the basis of my father's reputation; because of his status in the community, I could have obtained things that I would not have been able to get, otherwise. But I did not want to put myself in that position. I thought, "I am my own man and will have to do it on my own." So I could not buy a house.

My wife's parents offered us a flat to live in at no charge. I finally accepted, but I was very uncomfortable about this situation. And I knew that I would never be able to own a house in Iran.

Another problem was that I had to deal with a new lifestyle (new for me, since I had been young when I had left), and I felt like a stranger. Granted, I spoke the language, but I did not know my way around the system. And believe me, you needed to know your way around the system!

One of the defining things about life in Iran was the tightness of family. But now that I was here as an adult and a family man, I discovered that the tightness of family in Iran came with a lot of other expectations that I was not ready for—primarily, control. There were so many people in our family—grandparents and parents, and my wife's uncle, and my aunt, and so on. We were expected to respect a lot of people's input in our life. This, I was not OK with.

At last, I could not take it anymore. I thought, "I am not happy, I don't feel appreciated at work, and I don't feel welcome. If they don't appreciate what I can do and am doing to be a productive part of this company, they don't deserve having me!" And that was that.

Have you ever had the feeling that you are ready to give, but the one you want to give to isn't ready to receive? I felt there was so much more that I could do to help better myself as well as the community, but they couldn't take it in. I had tried every opportunity to make a difference, but I was not willing to sell my soul, to bypass what I had worked hard to become—a decent human being—in order to climb the ladder of success. It was not even about *my* success—it was about our community's success. I knew that I would not feel I had accomplished anything if it came at the cost of someone else's loss. Stepping all over people to get where you want is not for me.

So we packed up our bags and went back to America. And we have lived here ever since—by now, for over thirty years.

THREE GENERATIONS IN AMERICA

Once back in the United States, I had to get a green card. I had to start a new job, buy a house, and so on. I had to work to support my family. No longer a young student, I now had responsibilities. Then came the revolution.

Visit http://PersiaToTehrangeles. com/resources to get a feeling for the Iranian Revolution.

Then, unexpectedly in 1979, my parents came to live here, too. Then my wife's parents came. So within a short time, we were three generations together in America—my wife and I, our respective sets of parents, and our children. And our parents needed a lot of attention. They had a right to this: they had given us a lot of attention when we were living in

Iran, and now we had to return the favor. I had expected this to happen at some point; I just didn't expect it to happen so fast. Both sets of parents were financially self-sufficient, thank God, but they still needed a great deal from me. Yet I made a difference in their lives, and I am proud of this. Everyone in my immediate family and my wife's family was safe and had a future ahead of them.

This life-experience, as well as my having ample time to reflect on what we went through, has motivated me to write this book and share its findings with you. As a native-born Iranian living in the U.S. for more than three decades, I have been directly involved in the lives of three generations of Iranians in America. I know the struggles and the triumphs of each of these generations. And I can speak the language of each one well enough, I trust, to represent their situation to you.

How will this benefit you? Well, if you are an Iranian from the older generation in another country (such as the United States), you will see a compassionate view of your situation: what you had to go through in leaving your homeland and trying to get used to the very new American ways. And you will learn something about your grandchildren's generation from the middle, or "sandwich" generation—my generation—who had to bridge the past and future generations. This was my role for a long time.

If you are an Iranian of my generation living in the U.S. or another country, you may find relief at your own challenges being echoed by my experience and observations. You may be grateful to have a voice that can express your experience for you, here—a voice you can share with your friends, your older relatives, or your children.

If you are a child born in this country of Iranian parents, and identify yourself as Iranian-American, you can come to understand what challenges your parents and grandparents faced, and how—in my case, at least—your parents supported many of your new ways in the new world, even at the expense of their own comfort.

If you are not Iranian but are marrying an Iranian-American, you will learn a great deal about what your spouse has been formed by, and also many of the customs and traditions underlying what happens in the family that may have mystified you so far.

And for every reader, it is my fervent hope that the ways of the old world, and the still-becoming ways of the new world, may have a place in your awareness, and thus a way to be spoken of in conversation, as a result of this book. That way, nothing precious from the old world will be lost. And at the same time, what has yet to be from the new world will have room to become.

WHAT MIGRATION ASKED OF THE EMIGRES

What was it like for those who migrated from Iran to come here, and have their children grow up here? What were their reasons, their dreams, their challenges and obstacles, and the ways in which they moved forward? What is involved in leaving a culture with very unique and specific ways— not only beliefs, but down-to-the-fingernails details like how foods are cooked, how visiting of relatives and friends is done, the rhythms involved in working, eating, gathering together, and praying—and finding oneself in a brand-new culture with different ways, a different language, and often, different goals? What customs and traditions translate, and which get left behind?

And what about the children who are raised here by Iranian parents (and sometimes, grandparents)? How much of their culture do they get to keep, when they are pulled in two directions—expected to be Iranian at home but American at school? When at home, they breakfast on *halim* (wheat and turkey or beef cooked together with sugar and honey), *nano-panier* (bread with feta cheese or jam and butter), and soft-boiled eggs, but eat American food in the school cafeteria? How are they to integrate where they came from and where they are now? What got kept, in the process, and what got lost along the way?

These questions may apply to immigrants of almost any nationality, as they seek to find a new footing, better chances for their children, and a way to remember what meant so much to them in the land they left behind. But since Iran is the country I came from, I will focus on those who came here from Iran and the families who carried forth their legacies.

So thank you for coming along with me on this journey of exploration and understanding. Whether you think of yourself as an Iranian from the old country or Iranian-American; whether you are marrying or wanting to be close to someone with this rich cultural background; or whether you simply want to understand the Iranian culture and people better, you will benefit greatly from learning about the journey "From Persia to Tehrangeles."

In this chapter, first we'll talk about the older generation of Iranians who have moved to the Unites States and other countries. Then we'll focus on the newer generations, their children, and the challenges they face. Finally, we'll discuss the challenges and opportunities of non-Iranians who have married into these families.

THE OLDER GENERATION OF IRANIANS WHO MIGRATED TO AMERICA

The older generation of Iranians was not always the first to come to a new country such as the U.S. Sometimes they came because their children were here. In my case, this is what happened—though not in a planned-out way, as you will see.

There were a number of reasons why people of the older generation migrated to the United States (or another country, such as Turkey, England, and many others). Here are the most frequent reasons:

1. *They had a job in Iran that transferred them elsewhere.*

Many of the positions held in Iran were in the government. The government might transfer people with such positions—for instance, as an ambassador—to another country for many years. No one wants to live without their family for that length of time, so the government employee would take his whole family with him, and his children would grow up in the new country. This was generally a fairly easy move, in material terms, with the government helping with the costs and details of the relocation. So while the move required a transition, it was not a wrenching, rootless experience to come to the new country.

2. *They did not have a job in Iran, but they did have grown children who lived elsewhere, so they followed their children to the other country.*

This category fits those in the older generation in Iran who were well-off, financially, but who—naturally, wanting the best for their children—sought a better future for their children somewhere else. So they would send their children to another country: for instance, to go to a prestigious school. Later, they would follow their children there, as a family.

3. *They weren't happy in Iran, and wanted to make a new start.*

It's a different experience altogether to move to another country by choice because you think it will better your and your children's lives, than it is to move to another country because you see no other choice. This latter situation was the case with many Iranians over the last thirty or so years. Many moved elsewhere after the Islamic Revolution in 1979 because they were unhappy in Iran. Some were forced to move because of their religion, the position they held in the government, or other restrictions placed on them. Others realized that if they didn't move right away, their lives at home would become intolerable. So while this group made the choice to move, it wasn't actually a free choice as much as a survival choice.

To get out of the country most easily and affordably, some people started moving to nearby countries, such as Turkey. Those who could afford it, however, went to faraway countries such as the United States or England. This was the larger statistic, a statistic staggering in its implications when you consider that there are a million and a half Iranians in the United States, alone.

Yet there also is value in having to make the best of what life hands you, a Persian philosophy that was bred into me early. During *Norooz*, the Persian New Year, there is a ritual where an elder gives each child a holy book (in my family's case, the Qur'an) to open up at random, in which money has been hidden beforehand, tucked into certain pages. As a child carrying out this ritual, I might open to a page containing (the American equivalent of) $1, $5, or $10. I was taught to be satisfied with whatever portion I received; that it was God's gift to me, and to be thankful for it. Likewise, I was taught to be satisfied with the verse to which the money on the page pointed, which was viewed as my guidance for the coming year.

So with all these generations now living in the United States, I had to learn to adapt; and this made me flexible. I had to translate for my family, from one culture to another; and this helped me understand each generation and seek to help them understand each other. Accepting as my portion what had been given, yet seeking to bring the positive to the situation as best I could, helped me see what needed to be preserved (for example, the external and internal house-cleaning in readiness for the new year, one of the many rituals of *Norooz*) and what could be let go in favor of the new environment's ways (for example, letting my children have a Christmas tree because this was the common world of their schoolmates).

But in the beginning, this adaptation was not easy. It presented many challenges, and it sometimes called on strengths I didn't always think I had. Looking back, however, I see that I have come to enjoy a good life, dedicated to the service of others; that my children have found their way in the new world. For this reason alone (although there also are others), it was worth it to undergo the trials that came with the experience of migration.

Still, some things that are beautiful and meaningful from the old world didn't sufficiently make it into the new world. And that is also part of what I hope to remedy by sharing this book with you.

"We Came As Visitors…."

But I want to bring this story closer to home—to my own family, because I know their case so well that I can zoom in with a close-up lens to give you a closer look into this migration of the older generation and the adaptations it required.

In my parents' case, my father was a high-ranking officer in the Iranian army when the 1979 Islamic revolution started. At the time, he and my mother were here in the U.S. on vacation. They were visiting me, my wife, and our children. Suddenly, he and my mother could not go back; and, given the situation at home, they didn't want to. But they lost everything that they had back home: every piece of furniture, every family heirloom, every piece of clothing they had not packed in their suitcase. Their real estate, their other assets. Fortunately, they had some money. But still, imagine: you're on a family fun-visit for what you think will be a little while; and then find you cannot go back to the home where you have lived all your life, where your ancestors have lived all their lives. It's not just your furniture and land that are left behind; it's truly your soul.

"We came as visitors," my parents said. "Now we are residents."

And before long, my wife's parents also arrived.

Now they all would have to adapt to the new situation. It would be a challenge—for me as well as for them.

For one thing, they did not speak any English.

Needing To Learn The Language

My parents and my wife's parents were both here, now, and none of them spoke English. In addition to their survival being based on being able to speak the language, they also needed to learn the new country's customs and way of life. This might have been a challenging transition for anyone, but it was quite taxing for this generation—people of retirement age, some of whom had never been exposed to a different culture.

To learn the English language, many émigrés of my parents' generation took Adult Education classes, since they were too old for regular school. This had a double advantage: not only would they begin to learn to speak the language, there, but they often met other Iranians like themselves, as well as immigrants from different countries.

But learning to speak English did not happen overnight.

Needing To Get Around

Another question that quickly arose was, "How will they get around?" How would they do all the things they had so easily done in the old country—shop, go to the doctor's, do what they needed to do to live their lives?

Because my wife and I were in command of the language, we were pressed into service. We had to make all the arrangements to drive our parents where they needed to go. Wanting to help them be independent of us, we had to teach them to drive so they could get their own licenses. They didn't speak English yet, and the written test for the driver's license was only in English. (These days, it has progressed: the Department of Motor Vehicles is set up to administer the written test in Farsi, Arabic, and other languages. The American government has since realized that it needs to adapt to include people from other countries—such as China, Spanish-speaking cultures, Iran, and so on. But at that time, the test was in English, only.) Eventually they were able to get their driver's licenses; but all that involved an immense amount of work, time, coordination, and juggling other priorities such as work and family, on my part.

Needing To Be Able To Cook Familiar Foods

Food is one of the most binding elements of anyone's culture. And when you can no longer cook and eat as you are accustomed, the culture shock definitely sets in.

So another challenge for Iranian newcomers to this country was adapting to the way of cooking, here. Most of the foods they were used to back home weren't available here. America did not easily provide them with shops where they could buy the ingredients for making foods like *kale-pacheh* (the foot and head of lamb); *nano-panier*, *naan-sangak*, or *lavosh* (Persian breads); *tahchin* (saffron rice with chicken); and much more. They could not just walk out to the shops and buy fresh ingredients for making *khoreshte-gormeh-sabzi* (herb stew). They could not find a place to buy a traditional *samovar* for brewing their tea and keeping it going all day long.

See what was missing—for example, our Persian *Sofreh*. http://FromPersiaToTehrangeles.com/resources.

In addition, those who were from a very religious background required yet another adjustment regarding food, since they could not easily find butchers who slaughtered the animal in a way that was *halal* (permissible by Islamic law).

Eventually, this situation would get better, as the Iranian population increased. Los Angeles, for example, came to have so many Iranians living there that the area of Westwood was referred to as "Tehrangeles."

There, Iranians had their own stores, restaurants, and a number of large Iranian markets.

Needing A Place To Live

Many people who came here from Iran were used to having their own homes, as my parents and my wife's parents had. What were they to do, once in the United States, if they could not afford to buy their own homes? Sometimes, they moved in with their children.

Luckily, my parents were well-off, financially. They didn't need any help from us, and they could afford their own homes. But both my parents and my in-laws wanted to live close to us. It's natural, when you're new in a place, to want to live near somebody you know.

This meant that my wife and I had to choose a neighborhood where we could all live close together in the San Francisco Bay Area, and then help both sets of parents find a house. Fortunately, this came to pass. But it all took a great deal of time.

Making Adjustments, And Lingering Challenges

Gradually, things got better for newcomers. My parents had their own house and car, and things became somewhat easier for them. My mother could not speak the language properly, but she passed her driver's license test and had no problem getting around. Not only did she do her own shopping, but she often did our shopping, too. And my father was retired, so he didn't need to work.

I was the only one who was working. My wife stayed home and took care of the children. My parents babysat for us and helped us bring up our kids, taking them to and from school, as we helped them by taking them to the doctor and other places they needed to go. So everyone helped everyone else, when they could.

Homesickness

Still, my parents and others of the older generation were very homesick. It was difficult for them to adjust to life here when they came from a tight-knit community back home and couldn't do many of the things they were used to doing in Iran.

The language barrier had much to do with this. They missed speaking to each other in Farsi. They missed gathering with their friends. They missed going out where they had liked to go—to shop, to a concert, to other places. They simply missed their home in Iran and everything that went with it. I had basically grown up here since the age of seventeen, so it was easier for me to adjust. But for my parents, it was hard. So I had to help them.

Being Over-"Extended," and the Solution of Community

My parents expected a replica of what they'd had back home—such as places to go, relatives to visit with. Now, they expected us to entertain them, and to give them the attention they missed. Now that they were here, they didn't have anything to do. They sat at home all day. Watching TV was a limited option, because of the language barrier, but how much TV could they watch? My father tried to keep himself busy reading books, and my mother with shopping and cooking. Still, they had so much time on their hands that they didn't know what to do; while I had so much to do that for me there were too few hours in the day.

So my wife and I were quite busy, taking care of our big family. My parents wanted and deserved more attention, but they needed to be patient. I could not give them attention to the extent that they wanted. I had to work to support my family.

And I wasn't alone in this. Many of my friends were in a similar situation.

And then—together—my friends and I had a brainstorm.

We worked to get all our parents together to form their own community. "Why not?" we realized. "They're all in a similar position. They all miss the same foods. They all speak Farsi. Why not?" So we introduced them to one another. This made our lives much easier, and my parents' generation's lives much happier.

The communities began to form and take root. Now, my friends and I had our own community; my parents had their own community; and even my children and my friends' children got together and had friends to play with.

This is how the communities started. It made things so much easier for everyone. One of the virtues of having community is having others to share your lives with. Now they had friends to talk to, visit with, and do things with. The women exchanged recipes; the men talked about politics. So each family came to discover that they were not alone; that others also had similar problems, and that maybe some of these could be resolved together. The more friends they had, the busier they were, the less time they had on their hands, and the happier they were.

The more my parents were involved with their new friends, the more time my wife and I had to ourselves. And gradually, my parents became much less demanding and things started to get easier. People were discovering how much better community made their lives.

Gradually, the older generation adapted to the new environment. They had no choice but to accept all that was going on. And acceptance has a lot to do with happiness, because if you accept the situation you are in, you are happy with what you have.

As these Persian communities started to grow, they began blending with American culture and adapting to it. My wife and I had American friends who would come to our house and taste our food. We would get to know one another. My wife and I wanted to be accepted as part of the larger community, not just as members of the Persian community.

A LOOK AT THE WORLD THAT WAS LEFT BEHIND

To give you a sense of the older generation's homesickness and what it was like for them at first in this country, let me share the following story with you.

I will never forget the day my sister phoned me at work: "Mom is in trouble," she said. "She's lost control. She has locked herself in the closet, crying like crazy. Can you go to her right away?"

So I left work and went to my mother's house. Just as my sister had said, my mother was in the closet crying her eyes out.

"What is it?" I asked her, deeply concerned for her welfare.

She was crying so hard that it took her a while to get the words out. Finally, by listening to the fragments of sentences she choked out between sobs, I was able to make sense of the story: she had just heard that her much-loved younger sister had passed away back in Iran.

It took me hours to calm her down. "I want to go back," she wept. "I want to be there for the burial. I hate it here. I miss my country, I miss my family, I miss the way we do things there. I miss the traditions, the ceremonies, the love, the care, the tightness of my family. I have nobody here. I am tired of being alone."

It was hard for me to see my mother so helpless and hopeless, especially since I felt she had the *right* to be so unhappy. After all, Persian traditions and customs were the foundation of my parents' lives.

And so for my mother's sake, in the shortest time possible, I did my best to create a ritual for my aunt here that resembled the ceremonies done back home for the loss of a dear one. It helped her grieve her loss and make peace better than if I had done nothing that called up the old ways.

But my mother still missed her country and its customs. Whenever it came time for a major tradition, custom, or ceremony to take place back in Iran—Ramadan, Persian New Year, or some other—we would hear the same refrain over and over: "I wish I was back home."

There was no way I could tell her she was wrong in feeling this. There *was* something to be missed—something ancient and meaningful, comforting and vitalizing, ordinary and yet often sacred.

So at this point, before continuing the story of Iranian immigrant life in America among the generations, I would like to share with you an intimate picture of what the older generations missed.

Chapter 2

PERSIAN TRADITIONS, CEREMONIES, AND NON-RELIGIOUS CEREMONIES

A WORD ON TRADITION

There are three important life passages in Persian culture, my mother always said: birth, marriage, and death. I missed them all.

In my large extended family back home, I missed the birth of so many new babies, I missed so many weddings, and now I had to miss the opportunity to directly honor my aunt, and suffer the loss of someone so dear to me without benefit of these ancient and comforting rituals. I have tried to replicate these traditions here, but no matter how much I try, they will not be the same as they were back home, where the entire community participated.

In Persian culture ("Persian," here, refers to the ancient culture, while "Iranian" refers to the more modern culture), ceremonies play an important role, providing a way for everyone to get together, talk about their experiences or undergo some healing action, and support each other. Persians have always had close-knit families.

The way things have been done as a community or a nation over a period of many years constitutes what we call tradition. These ways may change over time, but they always contain a touch of the past. Persian traditions go back a great many years. Some are still in force, today. Yet though others have fallen by the wayside, it is good for a people to know where they came from so that they have all the more reason to move forward. And for those in this country who find these traditions completely new, still there may be something that moves the soul and tickles the fancy.

In this chapter you will learn about Persian:

- Burial
- Bath houses
- Tea houses, and
- Strength clubs (*Zor-khaneh*).

You will also find out about some *non*-religious ceremonies (religious ceremonies are detailed in the chapter on "Religion"):

- Seasonal and elemental festivals (the Winter and Autumn festivals, and the Water and Fire festivals)
- Rosewater, as it is used in ceremonies, and
- The tea ceremony.

THE BURIAL CEREMONY

Of the three important life passages that people celebrate in the Persian culture (birth, marriage, and death), only death is not viewed as a celebration of life. It could be, of course. But the Persian culture did not view it in this way. When somebody died, people would cry and kick themselves, jump up and down, and pass out.

I recall, as a child, becoming quite upset when my grandfather passed away. I couldn't comprehend why he was gone, and I missed having

I made a video that you can watch, in case you are ever in a similar situation. http://PersiaToTehrangeles.com/resources.

him around, sitting in his lap. At the memorial service, I noticed the sorrow of the many people who were gathered to pay their respects to my grandfather. I didn't understand about birth and death, then. I wondered what it was all about.

This is how death is treated in traditional Persian culture.

The Memorial Service (*Marasem Kakh Separi*)

In Iran, there are many people with different religions, each with their own ceremonies and events. But since the dominant religion is Islam, we will go into the Islamic memorial service, here. The memorial service as a whole is called *marasem kakh separi*. There is a deep religious underpinning to all the rituals.

When somebody passes away, in our culture, there are many things that need to take place in a very precise way. It takes a lot of work on the part of the surviving family, friends, and community. Everyone works together.

The Historical Tradition of Burying the Dead on Their Own Land

In early Iranian history, there were no cemeteries; and as people's worth was determined by how much land they owned, the tradition was to bury the dead on their own land. The issue of sanitation was not known about, then.

Nowadays, we do have memorial parks, and people have a choice about where they want to bury their loved ones.

The Burying Process (Kaf-no-dafen)

The process of the burial is called *Kaf-no-dafen*. The person who has died is called *meyet*. This is the Persian word meaning "no body, just a soul."

Addressing the Body

When a person passes away, the first thing that needs to be done is to address the body (that is, wash it, cover it, and so on). This intimate act is done by someone who was very close to the deceased person. If the deceased is a woman, then women address the body; no men can be around. If the deceased is a man, then men address the body, and there are no women around.

Those attending the deceased wrap the *meyet's* jaw shut, close the eyes, and cover the body with a sheet.

The Timing of the Burial After Death

In Islamic religion, you have only a short time in which to bury the deceased in a grave. The Qur'an says that the departed must be taken to the mosque or memorial ground just hours after dying, and not be left at home for days.

So, shortly after the person's death, the survivors call the ambulance to take the departed directly to the mosque or cemetery. Even if someone becomes gravely ill suddenly and has to be taken to the hospital, the hospital has a special holy room for this purpose (like a mosque).

The burial procedure is so delicate that it must be followed precisely. The rationale for this exacting ritual and precise timing is that otherwise, the person would not get to the other side on time to meet those whom he or she is supposed to meet there.

Division of Responsibilities

Because there is so much to do at such a time, the responsibilities are divided up among the surviving family, friends, and community. One person is responsible for taking care of the burial. Another person is responsible for the ceremonies and memorial. Another buys the grave, if it hasn't already been purchased in advance.

Usually, though, it has been. Most often, the person had bought it himself or herself while alive, aware that there would be so much to get done in such a short time, after death. My grandparents, for example, not only bought their own graves, but they even put money aside for tipping the person who would be washing them after death. My grandmother kept this money in her *kofan* (the seamless cloth the body is wrapped in). She told me, when I was young, "I want to spend my own money for the burial. I don't want anyone else to spend their money."

Another reason for buying your own grave is because the cost of grave plots tends to appreciate over time. As a friend of mine once said, "The most money I made in real estate was on my grave."

Taking the Deceased to the Memorial Park and Getting the Body Ready for Burial

The departed is then taken to the memorial park where his or her grave is. Each memorial park has its own bath house. This is because, in our religion, you have to wash the dead.

There are so many proper things you have to do:

1. The deceased must be positioned so that his or her feet are toward *Gableh*—the house of God.
2. A *mullah* (clergyperson) prays to God, while the helpers get the departed ready.
3. They pray the prayer *Namaz* (see the chapter on "Religion"). Then they read from the Qur'an and ask for the deceased's soul to be free, and for God to forgive the person so the soul can feel at home when it gets to the other side.
4. Then the body is washed. The *mordeh shoor* is a man or woman who is responsible for washing and cleaning the body, and preparing it to be put in the grave. The place where the person is washed is called *mordeh shoor khoneh*.
5. The body is wrapped in a seamless white cloth (white for purity) with verses of the Qur'an on it. This cloth is called the *kofan*. The *kofan* is used for this purpose, alone. For women, the *kofan* also covers their face (no one is supposed to see a woman's face). This veiling happens after the cleansing and praying has happened and the body is placed in the grave.

Putting the Deceased into the Grave

Before putting the *meyet* in the grave, a special prayer is done called the *Namaz meyet*. Then the *meyet* is placed in the grave wrapped in the *kofan*, with his or her feet facing *Gableh* (God's house). There is no coffin. The *meyet* goes back directly into the dirt which the body has come from. The belief is that nothing should be between the *meyet* and the dirt. (In some areas, this way of burial is not allowed, so a cardboard coffin must be used.)

All these rituals—the purifying cleansing, the *kofan* with verses of the Qur'an on it, the prayers, and everything else—are intended to prepare the deceased for the afterlife.

If the deceased is a woman, then a relative—a son, a father, or an uncle—called a *mahram* comes to put the woman (who is veiled) in the grave. The *mahram* is someone who was so closely connected to the deceased in life that the deceased's face does not need to be covered in front of him. Once the deceased is resting in the grave, the *mahram* unveils her face, which he alone sees. Then he gets out, and she is covered with dirt.

Wearing Black at the Service

Everyone has to wear black at the burial service. Afterwards, the immediate family wears black for at least 40 days, because they are in mourning. (*Aza* means being in mourning.) Wearing black means that you are in a lot of sorrow and pain. It is a way of saying, "I am in deep darkness and sorrow because I have lost you."

After the 40 days, a family elder brings a piece of colored cloth to the person whose loved one has died and asks that person to put it on. If a man has lost his wife, the elder will bring him a white shirt. If a woman has lost her husband, the elder is the mother-in-law or father-in-law. After this, the family can stop wearing black.

The Gathering

Now the gatherings begin. They usually are done in four phases:

1. The night before the third day—*Shabeh savom*: A place is rented in a mosque or a hall (usually, a mosque). When someone passes on, part of the mosque is reserved for this purpose. Tea and *halva* (saffron "brownies"—saffron with wheat flour, butter, sugar, etc.—a special treat for this occasion) are served. People cry and mourn for a few hours. Then everybody leaves. Men and women are separated during this time.

2. The night before the seventh day—*Shabeh haft*: At this time, people go to the grave and pray again for the departed's soul to be free. It's a very important night for the deceased, because this is when the soul will be questioned about how he or she has done in this world in order to be allowed to enter the next one. During this ceremony, the *mullah* stands by the grave and recites the *Namaz meyet* for the departed one. *Ghary* is the term for the praying and the words that are recited when the deceased is in the grave. *Ghary-khon* is the person who actually does the praying or singing.

All these restrictions existed because, in those days, there was no police, and people had to police themselves. So religion took on that role: "Do this, don't do that." You had to be a good person all your life, so you could go to heaven. Otherwise, according to the religious strictures, you would go to hell.

After the visit to the grave, a feast is served in the reception hall. This is supposed to be a celebration of life. This feast includes dinner, tea, and sweets (*halva*). People do their best to comfort the survivors.

However, some people, including me, feel that it's good to have this kind of celebration for a person when they're still alive. Sometimes people who know they are terminally ill actually convene a gathering to celebrate their life when they are still alive; then, after their death, there is no big celebration. This is a current custom among Iranian-Americans. For myself, I would prefer to find out if I made a difference in people's lives while I'm still here, rather than when I'm gone.

3. 40 days after passing—*Shabeh chaleh*: This is very much like the seventh day. Mostly the immediate family goes to the grave, at this point. The family may or may not decide to serve dinner. If they do, they invite everyone to their house.

4. One year after passing: At this point it's just the immediate family that goes to the deceased's grave. After paying respects, many families will have dinner afterwards. It's an opportunity to get together, eat, and converse.

To get a better picture of this ceremony, see: http://PersiaToTehrangeles.com/resources.

And Nowadays…

Nowadays, we can't expect people who have been exposed to a new culture to do things the same way as in this old custom. For example, I can't dictate that my children have so many ceremonies for me. I want to give them a choice, rather than telling them what to do.

In the old culture, people would put in their wills how they wanted the ceremonies and arrangements to be dealt with, after they passed on. But I want what's in *my* will to be for the sake of the people who are left behind, not that they should do something for me. The older generation felt that having a lot of things done for them after their death meant that they were good parents. To me, however, respecting people has more to do with how you treat and appreciate them in life than it does with having ceremonies for them after they have passed away. What's the point of disrespecting your parents while they are alive, and then making a fuss once they're dead?

I believe that the new generation has a right to do whatever they want. The easier I make things for them, the happier they will be to remember me. They'll remember the love I left behind, not the will I left behind that gave them no money but had a list of do's and don'ts. Life is about what you do when you're here. Everything you do should be in response to the question, "What am I here to do before I leave?"

Since you cannot take anything with you on this journey—since you have to leave everything behind—make sure that what you leave behind is what *should* be left behind. For instance, you could leave behind you a legacy of envy, jealousy, and negativity. Or you could leave behind a legacy of beauty by being generous, treating people right, and using well the gifts you have been created for.

When I go, I hope I won't need anyone to do anything for me that they don't want to. I hope I will have been so generous with my feelings that the people in my life feel loved and cared for by how I was with them while I was still alive. We should give thanks by sharing, and give love by caring about them while we are alive. If we do everything we should do, in life, then there will be no sorrow when we leave. Then it is a true celebration.

When a person is mean, often people cannot wait for that person to die. But wouldn't it be better to see that you really made a difference in someone's life while you were here? I believe that *this is the essence of the process of burial: to bury all the negative things while you are here*; to "bury the hatchet" before going into the grave, yourself. Then, when it's time for you to be in the grave, all that has to be put in there is your body; the positive memories of you live on forever. *The people who really die are those who have never lived. The people who live are the ones who leave something good behind.* A full life means that you have lived a good life for others. You're leaving everything behind, after all; so make sure that what you leave behind is worth leaving behind.

Life is a journey, and it's up to each of us to make it beautiful. Our attitude towards life, the way we treat other, will create for us either heaven or hell. I have always found that giving will elevate me to a higher level of my being. On the other hand, being bitter and unappreciative toward others brings me down to a level where I have trouble living with myself.

Let us respect everyone for their beliefs, and allow them to rise to their own level. Not everyone is the same in their beliefs and actions. Distance yourself from those who do not respect your beliefs, and try to be around those who give you respect. Don't criticize people for their actions but try to learn from them. Life is a learning process.

As I always encourage people, do what you want, but be aware of the cost of your actions. Be willing to face the consequences. Here are some guidelines you might consider adopting:

1. Don't walk all over everyone else to get to the finish line in life. You will win the race, but lose your humanity.
2. Walk through your life instead running through it. Smell the flowers and treasure every moment. It will never come back.
3. Respect people for who they are, not for who you want them to be. Have respect for those who do not follow your ways and appreciate your reasons. *There is only one leader, and that is God. We are all followers.*
4. Don't try to lead anyone else if you don't know where you're going. Don't even start walking until you know where you are going. A leader who is lost is like a bus to nowhere. Always try to remember where you are and where you are going. Have faith and trust yourself. You are here for a reason.

The Public Bath House

In the old days in Iran, people did not have bathing facilities in their houses. Therefore, they had to go to public bath houses. In the beginning, there was only one bath house for the whole neighborhood; so since men and women went to the bath house separately, on some days of the week the bath house was reserved for men, and on other days it was reserved for women. Over time, men and women could go together on the same day, but in different *nomreh* (private reserved rooms in the more expensive type of bath house, as distinct from the larger, more public one).

Check out some pictures of public bath houses: http://PersiaToTehrangeles.com/resources.

Kinds Of Bath Houses

There were two kinds of bath houses: *kahazineh* and *nomreh*.

Khazineh was like a big pool where everyone would jump in and wash themselves. People didn't know one another, and it wasn't always that sanitary (there could be viruses floating around), but going to the *khazineh* was cheaper than the other kind of bath house, the *nomreh*. *Khazineh* was also a place to meet people and exchange information. In those days, the way to get things done when you were out in public was word-of-mouth. Lots of deals were made in public places.

Nomreh was the other kind of bath house. Here, you would pay for a special private room that contained a shower and all the facilities. (*Nomreh* means "number." Each room had a number, as in a hotel.) I remember going there as a child with my father, sometimes. He took me because wanted me to know what it had been like before we had our own bathroom with tub and shower, which happened when I was about six.

Services, Customs, And Celebrations At The Bath House

One service that you could avail yourself of at a bath house was to hire a *daluk*. This was a person whose job was to bathe and massage you. It was a luxury to have this service; only wealthy people could afford it. When you rented a room at *nomreh*, you could bring as many people as you wanted, and the *daluk* would come and wash each person.

People who couldn't afford to hire a *daluk* would go to *khazineh*, where they often would wash each other. It was a literal case of "You scratch my back, I scratch yours." I never had a stranger scratching my back, because if there wasn't a *daluk* around, my father would wash my back, and I would wash his. As a child, I did not always enjoy the presence of the *daluk* because sometimes I only wanted to play and splash in the water. But the *daluk* whom my father had hired just wanted to do his job—to wash me and get out. I felt he was spoiling my fun.

Women usually spent all day at the bath house. I would go with my mother to the women's bath house when I was about three years old. We would have lunch there. But by the time I was four, I already was seen as too old to go with my mother, so I had to start going with my father to the men's bath house.

Reservations usually were required to go to the public bath. You would call a day ahead and give them a list of what you needed. Although you could rent a towel or buy a bar of soap, people generally took their own toiletries (towel, soap, shampoo, and so on) for sanitary reasons.

In those days you could also pay for room service. They would bring you towels, drinks, ice water, and so on (of course, they charged you for everything). There was no Coke or other soda in those days, but there was *limonade*, a colored drink in a jar.

The Bath House and the Wedding Process

Going to the public bath houses was also part of the Persian wedding process (as you'll see when you get to the chapter on "The Persian Wedding"). The people who were involved in this elaborate process usually would rent the entire bath house for themselves and their guests. This meant that could choose to go to either *kahazineh* or *nomreh*.

There usually was a bachelor party before a wedding. The groom's friends would take him to the bath house. They would pay for it, since he was the guest of honor. They could have any kind of entertainment, if they so desired, including singers and popular music. More religious people, however, either would have no music at all or else they would have religious music.

The bride also had a party at the bath house—usually, a much larger one than the groom's party.

At both the groom's and bride's parties, people sat around wearing a *loung* (a piece of fabric wrapped around them so they wouldn't be naked) and ate catered food.

For a bridal shower, a groom shower, or a baby shower, people either would rent part of the bath house or would rent the entire place.

Celebrating the Birth of a Child at the Bath House

When a woman was pregnant, she would go to the public bath before the baby was born. The public bath also was used seven days after a married woman had her first child, as a celebration. This was called *Hammom zayeman*—a baby's first bathing after birth. At this time, the father of the baby would *gorough* the bath house (reserve part or the entirety of the bath house, depending on how many guests they had). Then the mother and baby, the immediate female family and friends, and invited guests would celebrate the baby's birth. It was a big celebration. Lunch, fruits, and sweets were served. Some families brought in music and singers as part of this celebration.

After the bathing was done, everyone would go to the mother's house and continue celebrating—especially if the baby was a boy. In those days, it was considered a big thing for the first child to be a boy, because he would carry the family name.

And now, a humorous aspect of the old tradition: If a man and a woman had sex the previous night, before sunrise they had to cleanse themselves (*taharat*) by going to the public bath house prior to doing their daily prayers, *namaz*, at sunrise. Public baths were always open before sunrise. So at four in the morning, people were in the street. The couple would try to sneak out without anyone knowing, but everyone in the whole neighborhood knew that anyone who went to the bathhouses before sunrise had had sex the night before. The young kids, especially, would tell each other who "did it last night." There was no privacy when you lived in such a tight-knit community.

And In Our Time…

Nowadays, each house has its own indoor facilities (although in some areas of Iran, bath houses may still exist). We take so many things in our lives for granted, such as being able to shower or bathe as often as we want, to shampoo our hair and to brush our teeth. So the next time you take a bath, think of those who do not have this opportunity even once a month. Give thanks for where you are and what you have—all the things that have helped you be where you in life and become the person you are now.

Likewise, the old days of favoring boys over girls are gone. We all count our blessings for the arrival of a child of either gender. Let us thank God for the trust He has in us in giving us, as parents, this chance to nurture His creation. It is truly an honor to father or mother a child.

When I am asked what is the best achievement of my life, I always respond: *fatherhood*! When I look at my daughter or my son, I thank God for trusting me enough to give me this chance, and being on my side through it all.

TEA HOUSES

In the past, tea houses were an important part of Iranian culture. Tea houses were called *ghahveh-khaneh* (literally, *ghahveh* means "coffee," and *khaneh* means house). The tea house was the hub of social activity. There were tea houses all over.

Going to a tea house was considered a male activity. Men would gather together there and drink tea, and smoke cigarettes or *chopogh* (*hookahs*). The *chopogh* looked like a long pipe that contained tobacco. In more ancient times, the men would also smoke opium (which wasn't illegal, then.)

As a child, I often went to the tea house with my grandfather—never with my father; he had to work, so he never went to the tea house. Mostly, it was older men who went, since they were retired.

See pictures of traditional Persian tea houses. http:// PersiaToTehrangeles.com. com/resources.

The tea house was a place where a lot of personal interaction took place. People would get together and talk about their lives. Business would be conducted. A lot of businesses got their start, there. Many weddings also had their origins in tea-house conversations.

Tea houses were popular at a time before telephones or newspapers served as the media centers of the community. But now that we have more sophisticated ways of communicating with each other, tea houses play a greatly diminished role in Iranian culture.

And Nowadays…

These days, the new generation of Iranians goes to places like Starbucks, instead. They drink coffee, work on their laptops, and chat about their lives. And yet I'm sure a time will come when even Starbucks will become outmoded, because people will find something more up-to-date.

STRENGTH CLUBS (*ZOR-KHANEH*)

In the Western world, there is no exact equivalent of the "strength club" (*zor-khaneh*). Our closest match in modern times is probably a gym. But it's not really the same.

The *zor-khaneh* was a club where men went to become strong and show off their strength. (*Zor* means "strength," and *khaneh* means house; so *zor-khaneh* is a "house of strength.") Men would do pushups, lift weights, and so on. Wrestling was one of the big sports of previous generations. Even today, Iran is still known for wrestling in the Olympics and worldwide.

Peek into a *Zor-khaneh*. http:// PersiaToTehrangeles.com/ resources.

The Spiritual Aspect Of *Zor-Khaneh*

Almost everything that was done in Persian culture, no matter how seemingly secular, also had a strong spiritual aspect to it. So *zor-khaneh* wasn't only a place for men to exercise and compare their strength: it was also an institution of learning. Each neighborhood had its own *zor-khaneh*, which was headed by an older leader, a wise spiritual person who guided younger people who sought to learn. He was retired now, but once he had been known for his strength, similar to a gold-medal winner in the Olympics.

Everything that was done there was not random, but had a meaning. The leader sat on a special chair that was raised above everyone else, called *takht-gah*. No one ever sat in this place but him. People would kiss the ground in front of him before approaching, as a sign of respect. And every time someone of high standing walked in, a man would ring a bell and play the drum, as a sign of respect.

Each leader of a *zor-khaneh* had a successor lined up to take his place after he was gone—someone from the same neighborhood, who was well known at the club.

And In Our Time...
Like the tea houses, the *zor-khanehs* are fading away.

NON-RELIGIOUS CEREMONIES
Since many Iranians have moved to the United States or other countries, changes have taken place in many of the ceremonies, some of which were celebrated religiously and some non-religiously. I will go into the most important religious ceremonies in the chapter on "Religion." Here, I will discuss some of the more important non-religious ceremonies.

Seasonal And Elemental Festivals

Winter Festival (Shaba Yalda)
Shaba yalda is the longest night. In Persia, we celebrate because it means that the long dark nights are over and brightness is coming in. Just as we celebrate *Tir*, the longest day, we also celebrate the longest night.

This shows that there are always times for celebration. Life itself is a celebration. You just have to learn how to celebrate it.

Usually, the whole family would get together for *shaba yalda*. In those days, they heated the house in winter with *korsi*, a square table with coals underneath, in the middle of the family room. There were cushions around it and a big blanket on top, which everyone sat underneath to get warm. They slept there at night. *Korsi* was the main attraction of *shaba yalda*.

On *shaba yalda*, they ate watermelon for the express reason that it is hard to find in winter. There was a teaching in this. People eat watermelon all summer long,

See what it's like around the *Korsi*. http://PersiaToTehrangeles.com/resources.

but don't really appreciate it until the longest night of the year. Then they appreciate it more, because they know you really have to look for it in winter. So the point was to try to get something they usually didn't have, to understand that the time to appreciate what you have is when you have it.

In one of my poems, I say:

"What you don't have
Is the picture of something that you had some time ago.
But the darkness has taken over, and you don't see it."

If you appreciate what you have all the time, you won't miss it when you don't have it, because you have paid your respects and done justice to it. But if you take what you have for granted, then it takes a time when you don't have it—like watermelon at *shaba yalda*—for you to miss and appreciate it. That's how life is.

Autumn Festival (Jashne-mehregan)

The autumn festival is celebrated in the month of *Mehr*, the seventh month of the Persian year (equivalent to October in America). As it's very close to Thanksgiving, this is a time to give thanks for what we have. We celebrate the harvest of what we planted in the spring. So we thank God for what we have produced, and hope we will be able to produce even more the following year.

Whatever you have is a labor of love, because you have put a lot of labor into what you have planted. Now you are harvesting your labor of love. This will give you more desire to give, which will bring you even more, and more. It's not only about literally planting seeds in the ground. There are inner ways to plant seeds, too. If you plant the seed of love, then you harvest kindness, vitality, purity, and other virtues. It all depends on what you want to plant in life. Do you want to plant sadness, anger, and jealousy? Or do you want to plant kindness, generosity, and love?

Water Festival (Jashne-tirgan)

The water festival, *jashne-tirgan*, takes place in the month of *Tir*, the fourth month of the Persian calendar, on the longest day of the year. This used to be a very popular festival. However, very few people celebrate it any more, except in some parts of Iran.

Tir means "water," as well as "purity," and "lightness." The longest day means that the nights are getting shorter, and there will be more light. On this day, people get together, celebrate, and eat. Ceremonies are always an excuse to get together, gossip, and eat.

Fire Festival (Ghashne sade)

This is another festival that has become less popular than in the old days. It celebrates the discovery of fire, and is held in the middle of winter during *Behman*, the tenth month of the Persian year. People gather around a fire, and roast chestnuts and sometimes bake potatoes in the fire. Food is served, including fruits. In Persian culture, fruits are a way to show hospitality. Iranians, even those living abroad, always have a big bowl of fruit on their table whenever they are entertaining.

Rosewater In Ceremonies (*Golab-Giri*)

Golab-giri is the season when water is extracted from rose petals. Rosewater is very important in our culture. It is used for cooking, baking, as an air freshener, and also for perfume. My great-grandmother always used to sprinkle rosewater over herself, and it smelled wonderful. It was used in all the ceremonies—weddings, burials, happy and sad occasions. It was more popular than the Chanel Number Five my mother used.

Learn more about *Golab-giri.* **http://PersiaToTehrangeles.com/resources.**

The process of making rosewater is a ceremony in itself. People still take bus tours towards the end of spring to go and watch this process, which is quite involved and takes several days. Ghamsar, a place in Iran, is known for its rosewater. Everybody who goes on the tour comes out smelling like a rose.

Tea Ceremony

Tea represents Persian hospitality. If you go for a visit to an Iranian house, you will always be offered two things: first tea, and then food. Tea is brewing all day, until the family goes to bed.

In the old days, the woman of the house would get up in the morning and start the *samovar* for tea. The morning meal was always concluded with a glass of tea. A *samovar* is a metal container that holds water and has a cavity in the middle. Charcoal is heated until it is red, then it is put inside the cavity. This boils the water and keeps it warm. Then a teapot containing tea leaves is put on top of the samovar and covered with a cloth, so the tea can simmer.

To learn to make and serve Persian Tea, see: http://PersiaToTehrangeles.com/resources

Important Qualities of Tea

Tea comes from the northern part of Iran. These are there important qualities of tea: color, aroma, and taste. And of course, the overall quality of the tea is important, as well. The more expensive the tea, the better it tastes.

How Tea Is Served

The tea is always served in a small glass (*estekan*). Cardamom is usually used to flavor the tea, which is served on a tray with a spoon and a cup containing sugar cubes. People would place a sugar cube in their mouth, then let it dissolve by drinking the hot tea. Nowadays, tea is often served with sweets and is flavored with saffron or rosewater.

And Nowadays…

These days, all *samovars* are electric, so no coals are required. All you do is plug in the *samovar*, which has a teapot on top. You put in tea leaves, add hot water, let it brew in the *samovar*, and then serve the tea.

Still, if you look with a broad vision, you will see that the influence of other cultures is not necessarily a bad thing. The introduction of electricity into Iranian culture made the electric *samovar* possible.

In the United States, not every Iranian or Iranian-American has a *samovar*. In this generation, those who have to work full-time don't have time to brew tea with a *samovar*. Some use an electric glass container, which they plug in after adding tea leaves and water. Others just use a teabag and hot water. But with the wide variety of teas available now, anyone can enjoy a good cup of tea.

People drink tea in Iran as frequently as Americans drink coffee. If you like your tea strong, then you put less water into it. In Iran, we always drink our tea hot. This is what I prefer, even on hot summer days, which might seem strange to those Americans who like iced tea in the summer. It's all a matter of preference; either way is fine. And remember, enjoy your tea quietly; it's rude to make noise drinking tea.

BRINGING IT ALL TOGETHER

With the tightness of Persian communities in the old days came respecting the elders and those in authority. All the gatherings and ceremonies were for the purpose of bringing the families together.

Families, in our culture, are very tightly knit. This is a community where people associate not only with their immediate family but also with relatives such as second cousins, third cousins, uncles, aunts, grandparents, and children. When they got together at a family gathering, there might be as many as fifty people. Such gatherings and ceremonies were done publicly and would take place a few times a year, normally at the elder's house.

Respect for elders is important in our culture. You would never sit down in front of a respected person such as a spiritual leader or a grandparent unless you were asked to. You would always bend over and kiss the ground, in their presence, and never speak unless spoken to. People who were high in society—who were in government, spiritual leaders, or who were well-known for something they had done—were awarded this kind of respect.

The youngest in the family had a lot to put up with, since everyone was older. With age came wisdom, know-how, and respect. People would always go to their elders to ask for guidance, and for permission concerning significant matters, such as getting married, leaving the country, or doing something else very important. This was the respect you gave to your elders.

However, such respect often came from fear rather than from love. But that is not really respect. I want people to respect me because they think I deserve it, not because they're afraid of me. Real respect comes from the love you have for a person.

Although women were always supposed to be respected, in our culture, they were not respected in the proper way, because the man of the house made all the decisions. Women's rights didn't exist, in our culture. Neither did children's rights or human rights—except for those in authority. The rest of the people just had to obey the authorities, and were treated very disrespectfully.

So now that we Iranians have come to the United States and other countries, we see that women have authority. They have important things to say. And in Iran, as well, we have moved on to a more modern culture. Now, women have positions in the government and are artists, scientists, and much more.

Chapter 3

ADJUSTING TO
THE NEW WORLD

The Other Generations

When the older generation came here (Persian customs, traditions, and ceremonies still in their memories and in their blood), everything was different. And so acclimation was difficult for them; sometimes even painful.

One major example had to do with power in the family. In Iran, the men ran the household and the women obeyed. But when they came here, they discovered that women's liberation was a strong force. Women here didn't want to listen to their husbands all the time. They were developing a sense of their own being, and starting to feel good about themselves. They even had their own gatherings, which made the men feel left out.

Even the relationship to their children was not the same, here. After all, back in Iran, parents *told* their children what to do and how to live; and the children obeyed. But in this country, things weren't going that way. My generation had the option of raising their children differently. I, for one, took this option.

The older generation felt confused and disturbed by all this. To them, it probably felt like chaos was taking over. Every segment of this society felt pulled in a lot of different directions.

THE CHILDREN'S GENERATION— BEING "IRANIAN-AMERICAN"

The children of Iranian immigrants like me soon realized that things could be different for them in the new country. In Iran the father was the head of the household by fiat, and his children automatically obeyed. But here, children felt that they had a right to independence: to think for themselves and do as their American peers did.

This new opportunity did not make it easy, for them, however. They had their own special challenges adjusting to the new environment. Simply going to school in America changed things for our children. When they were out of their home, they led an American lifestyle; and at home, they had to conform to an Iranian lifestyle. It was really hard for them, trying to balance the two different cultures and having to lead double lives. Their parents might speak to them in Farsi at breakfast, but then the children would go off to school to encounter the American culture. If the girls wore headscarves according to the family's cultural way, they stood out among their schoolmates and teachers.

The children were learning a language and skills and ideas that their parents might have no way to relate to. Many of their parents didn't speak English. And it was embarrassing for the kids to have to tell their friends, "We're Muslim, we don't celebrate Christmas or New Year's." Or to be asked out on a date and have to respond, "I'm not allowed to be out with a guy" and do other things their friends always did.

What was a parent to do? You could try to keep the children in the house, sheltered and sequestered from the new lifestyle. But that wasn't really a choice. In America, all children have to go to school, or there are legal ramifications. There was no way around it: being exposed to different lifestyles in school, the children had a choice between the old ways and the new ways. And they chose the new, freer lifestyle because it made them happier.

As the middle generation between my parents and my children—the "sandwich" generation—I did not want to automatically impose all Iranian traditions on my Iranian-American children. I could see that the old ways of parenting in Iran were not always compatible with the new American ways. So my feeling was that some of the traditional conventions had to be turned around.

For example, when my daughter reached a certain age, she decided to date, just like her American friends. I accepted this. Since she had grown up in this country, and I myself had been educated here, I leaned towards bringing up my children in the freer style of this new culture. But my parents' generation could not understand these ways. My father was used to marriage Iranian style, where the prospective groom never even sees the bride until the day of the wedding ceremony (see "The Persian Wedding" chapter for details). My parents actually blamed me for how I was bringing up my children.

But I understood this new culture better than my parents did. I understood what my children were exposed to, and what it made them want. I knew how I wanted to raise my children: this did not include me *or* my parents telling my children how to live. Coming from their traditional culture, my parents were prepared to tell my children what to do all the time, and I needed them to learn that this wasn't how things were done here.

As a parent, I wanted my children to have the rights they deserved; and as a grown child of my own parents, I wanted my parents to understand what I was doing. To me, when a child is eighteen, he or she is an adult to be respected, not just someone to boss around. I felt it was more important for me to *learn* from my children and help them live their own lives, here, than to keep a custom going for its own sake.

I began to realize that parents from Iran like me, who had brought their children to this country, had to be the ones to adapt to their children's new lifestyle. As Iranian-American children got older, they wanted to belong to the new country more and more. They wanted to date, to hang out with their friends, to have their own phones and computers and so on. Later, they wanted go to college, to marry someone of their own choice, and generally to be much more independent than their Iranian counterparts got to be.

Generational Clashes

This is how many generational clashes started. The kids wanted to be on their own; but at the same time they needed their parents. And the parents tended to want to control their children's lives and not know what to do about this new situation. It was hard for them to understand their children's feelings. A lot of families actually went into therapy, seeking help in adjusting to this new scenario.

The children's challenge was: "How can I make my parents realize that we are not in Iran anymore?" And the parents' challenge was the fear of losing their culture. They were very attached to their roots and customs. "How can I call myself an Iranian," they thought, "if I don't even have Iranian customs anymore?" And they had a point. Everything is a custom—your religion, the way you eat, the way you talk, the way you associate with people—the whole lifestyle.

For example, Iranians who are Muslims do not eat pork. But their children here, exposed to new ways, might want to eat bacon. What is a parent to do? Back home, women have to wear a veil, a *chador*. Here, no one does. Women dress more provocatively than in Iran. What is a parent to do?

In our culture, you have to listen to everything your parents say. Here, although children respect their parents, they don't feel they have to obey them automatically. Here, at a young age, children here want to smoke cigarettes and drink—all the things that they're not supposed to do in traditional Iranian culture. In Iran, girls don't wear makeup until they're married, but here, they wear lipstick and nail polish at 12 years old. In Iran, boys don't bring girls home until they are married, but here, boys want to bring their girlfriends home at the age of 13, and the father doesn't want that. So these are two totally different worlds.

Here, the children are the ones to determine their own lives. They decide which university they want to go to. They decide that they don't want to live with their parents (a radical reversal of life back in Iran). Although children respect their parents and are proud of their roots, they don't want to bring their parents into their social circle, because their parents have accents and a different lifestyle. What the children want is to blend in with their friends, not to be tied to the old ways. So for me, I had to be in the background as a parent. In Iran, the parents were the center of attention.

The challenges intensified when my children were teenagers, here. Then the phone was the most important part of their life; they wanted to be on the phone all the time. I was very fortunate: while I sought to be an understanding parent, I also was able to discipline my kids. We maintained one phone line. But some of my friends my age, with children my children's age, gave in. They had three or four phone lines in the house, because their teenagers were on the phone all the time and each one had to have their own line.

See the video of me reciting a poem I wrote about this: http://PersiaToTehrangeles.com/resources.

Driving was another issue. Our kids wanted to have a car and drive as soon as they reached 18. I often told them, "Be careful. I know you'll follow the regulations, but there are other people on the road who won't." Many times my children would come home late, and my wife and I would stay up worrying about them. We had a lot of sleepless nights.

Now, our children are working and having their own families. They are at the age where they are facing their own challenges, like work and family. We had our parents to babysit the kids, but our children don't have that privilege because we, their parents, are still working. So it's tougher for our children. They have to put their children in daycare or preschool, or find a nanny.

MY GENERATION—THE "SANDWICH GENERATION"

In trying to simultaneously cope with my children's situations, deal with my parents and their needs, and manage my own life, I found myself sandwiched between two different cultures and generations. And so I began to think of myself as the "sandwich generation," a buffer between three generations and two different cultures and lifestyles. It often was exhausting, trying to give my parents what they wanted, satisfy my kids, and deal with the community as well. I felt pushed to the limit. Sometimes I couldn't help feeling, "What's the point of living?" I was trying to satisfy so many different needs and wants, and no one seemed to care about what *I* needed.

This affected my marriage, too. My wife and I were responsible for a larger family than most people in this country are. She had not only our kids to take care of, but also her own parents. And I had to be the buffer between my kids and my parents. We both had too much to do.

For example, in the beginning, when I came home from work, my parents expected me to entertain them because they had nothing to do all day. But I wasn't up for entertaining anyone. I had been working hard all day. Sometimes I would get home so late that I would even not see my kids, because they were asleep. So I was tired, after work. I just wanted to have a nice meal and relax, with no responsibilities.

Any good relationship is based on understanding, on give-and-take. But that didn't exist between the generations of our families, early on. It was hard for my parents to put themselves in my shoes as I attempted to raise my children more respectfully, because *they* had never listened to their kids. Today, Iranian grandparents in this country are still like that. They're always the ones telling you what they want. It was easier for my son, because he had me to understand his situation, whereas my parents couldn't empathize with mine.

It's hard to take the culture and lifestyle out of people; it's much easier to put it in them.

So as a buffer sandwiched in between two different generations, I needed a great degree of skill. I needed to know how to react to every situation, to all the forces coming from each side. I had to be able to understand everyone else's point of view, because if the buffer does his job right, both sides will end up being happy. I had to give up some of the things I wanted, but I learned to cope with it. Still, I wanted my life to be more than this. I thought, "Why do I have to live everybody else's life—my mother's life, my father's life, my wife's life, my kids' life. I want to live my *own* life!"

To hear my poem about this, see: http:// PersiaToTehrangeles.com/ resources.

I had to live my *wife's* life, because she was not as independent as an American woman. The same thing was true for my mother. There was so much pressure on me that I felt I could either have a breakdown or a breakthrough. And since I didn't want to have a breakdown, I learned to keep certain things to myself. I learned, for example, not to tell my daughter what I had heard from my mother's side, because she wouldn't like what my mother said. That's the job of the buffer: to filter everything you hear and see. It would have been much easier for me not to take on this role, but I assumed it because I wanted my children to lead a better life than I did. Since I brought my children to this country and exposed them to a new culture, I felt it was my job to allow them to grow into this new culture without being subjected to all the pressures from the old way of life.

One of the pressures from the old way of life my parents kept up was that they would come to my house unannounced. In Iran, you just went to someone's house when you felt like it, knocked on the door, and went in. But that custom was hard for me, here. When I come home from a day of hard work, I'm not *ready* to accept anyone into my house. My wife and I were tired. We didn't *feel* like having company. My parents and my wife's parents didn't understand this. They expected me to be happy and lively after working hard all day.

So the first custom that I deliberately adopted in this country was to call in advance before visiting, out of respect for the people in the house, to give them time to get ready. I would never go to my daughter's house and just walk in without having permission beforehand. Both my children know I respect them enough not to do that.

But the respect we're taught in our culture is automatic, not earned. There, when your father comes into the room, you get up and continue standing. When you're a child, he can come to your room without telling you, even if you have your pajamas on. So when he wanted to just walk into my home now that I was an adult, it no longer felt natural; it felt invasive. I wanted him to tell me he was coming, so that I could dress properly, act properly, and generally be prepared for his visit so that the visit wouldn't leave a bitter taste.

This is the kind of understanding people in families (and beyond) need to have about each other. My job, here, was to familiarize both generations with each other's culture in order for everyone to be able to live in harmony. My parents didn't have any knowledge of American culture, and my kids didn't have any real knowledge of Iranian culture. My daughter and mother loved each other, but they fought because they didn't understand one another. Both my parents and kids needed to learn that if you want to get your way all the time, you will get nowhere.

My parents didn't understand the pressures affecting me, and my wife didn't understand the situation my parents and hers were in. I didn't want my children's marriages to suffer like mine did from lack of flexibility and understanding.

It's all about understanding.

THE NEED FOR SOCIETAL UNDERSTANDING

The lack of understanding within a family can be reflected and exaggerated on a much larger, societal scale and cause a great deal of suffering. This was our experience as a people facing stereotyped prejudice.

As Iranians in America, we faced one of the biggest and most important problems during our life in the U.S. in 1979, during the hostage crisis—when the Iranian government of Ayatollah Khomeini arrested 52 Americans and held them captive for 444 days. At the time, I owned a restaurant here, in a non-Iranian American community. Because of the hostage crisis, just about everyone in the community boycotted our restaurant because I was Persian. I would greet people with the same good food and friendliness as before, but it got to the point where I had to explain to every customer who walked in that what was going on in my country had nothing to do with me. I told them, "I'm totally against what they're doing in Iran." But people were angry about the hostage situation, and so they hated Iranians.

This closed-minded and -hearted reaction made it very difficult to continue running the restaurant. I had expenses and overhead, and now I wasn't making any money. Some of my employees, high-school kids, quit because their parents didn't want them working for an Iranian, *any* Iranian. I had to put an American flag everywhere. I knew that not one Iranian living here was in favor of the hostage situation. But it did no good to say so. We were all being crucified because of the Iranian government's actions. Finally, I had to give up the restaurant.

The anger toward Iranians affected my children very deeply. In school, they were bullied and made fun of by the other kids. And I was affected because I was in touch with a lot of Americans, in my work and personally. Unfortunately, we are still in the process of trying to tell everyone that Iranians are a loving, caring people. Currently, many organizations are trying to promote the Persian culture and familiarize people with it, especially because of all the negative publicity we've been getting due to prejudice. These organizations are trying to prove that Iranians are not terrorists, as the stereotyping makes us out to be.

And this is the purpose of my writing this book and starting my "KShar's Kitchen" website to teach people how to cook Persian food: to keep my culture alive and to help people understand who we are as individuals.

THE BENEFITS OF BEING EXPOSED TO A NEW CULTURE

So far I have talked mainly about the challenges that every generation faces when exposed to a different culture. Now, let's take a look at the *benefits*. Because I think there are no losers in this story. We've all gained something valuable.

For The Older Generation

One benefit for the older generation of being exposed to another culture is that they get to learn how to be less attached to what they had before, instead welcoming what they met up with in the new place. People of my parents' age had to learn to overcome their many challenges and adapt to the new environment. Once they did, they could be thankful for what they had learned.

There were times when all of us got so frustrated coping with all the changes confronting us that we just wanted to give up. My parents got to the point where they felt, "It's too different. I'd rather go back home." But my father knew that if he went back home, he would be assassinated, so he had to stay here. He had no choice.

People like my father who had high-ranking jobs in government and business, back in Iran, suffered the most. There, although they had a lot of responsibility, they also had it easy, everything at their fingertips. They were well respected; they had so many titles before and after their name that they could have used a truck to carry them. He had assistants, people who would walk behind and in front of him, bodyguards, a chauffeur, everything. And for two of my four uncles, it was the same thing. So when my father came here, it was hard for him, because no one respected him. He was viewed as just an ordinary person. He had to mow his own lawn.

Back there, my father was an authority, with all those titles—like a god. Here, he was treated like a nobody. In Iran, you had someone shop for you; here, you had to do your own shopping. Back home, everybody would listen to you, as the man of the house. Men were very powerful in Iran; and now here, they were facing women's liberation. Women didn't put up with what they had put up with back home. They wanted to live their own lives; and this made for problems in my parents' generation. The men felt no one respected them, any more. In our culture, "respect" meant how much you could push other people around—like a bully.

So when my father first came to this country, he was depressed. He missed the power and respect he'd had before. But the respect was really a lot of hot air. Nothing real comes from it.

On the other hand, the Iranian women of that generation, like my mother, were very happy with these changes. They could voice an opinion; they didn't have all the limitations they'd had back in Iran. So even though they still had challenges, they liked it here.

Some among my parents' generation, here, were financially well off. But others had to support their families, often by working jobs they didn't like. Some people who'd had good jobs in Iran ended up driving taxis, here. Others, who were too old to find a job here and didn't speak English, had to start their own businesses, such as grocery stores and restaurants. But still, they were alive and meeting their challenges the best way they could.

Because it was so hard for our parents, to ease our consciences we would involve them in our everyday lives as much as we could. And once my parents' generation began finding people with whom they could visit, have parties, talk about their problems, and look for solutions—making their own friends—they felt less isolated and more supported in this new, challenging environment. They started realizing that although they missed a lot by not being in their native land, they also had learned so much more by being here that they wouldn't have otherwise. They grew to be a bigger person, and they learned to respect their children's and grandchildren's rights.

Now, they were acting as grandparents should. They appreciated their grandchildren and everyone more; they respected people in a proper manner; and they let everyone live their own life.

For My Generation

For my generation, we were able to have our own friends and gatherings and have a good time. Yes, we had to work hard to support our families; but because we were younger it was easier for us than for our parents to adapt to this new environment. Also, like me, many had lived here before and spoke English.

I was able to support my family and have a good lifestyle. We had our parents to babysit our kids and take care of them.

My generation experienced so much growth in understanding the situation that our parents were in and the situation that our children were facing. We learned to respect our old customs and lifestyle, at the same time appreciating the new direction that our children were going in life.

I believe that *every* generation needs to live in its own surroundings, and yet once in a while to take a leap of faith and step outside its comfort zone so it can experience and learn something new.

For Our Children's Generation

Despite the generational and cultural clashes that came with being of two cultures, eventually, my kids (and most others in their generation) went to college and ended up being productive citizens with decent jobs. Now they are attorneys, physicians, social workers, and more—a very respectable part of the Iranian-American community. Not only do they appreciate American culture, but they are also coming to appreciate where they came from.

So each of the generations has had its challenges. And each of us, individually, has either learned what we needed to learn and accepted change, or has not accepted it but has been compelled to live with it anyway. Those who haven't been able to embrace the new situation end up not being very happy. That's why I tell my friends and acquaintances that in order to be happy, we have to be able to understand the whole situation. One reason I'm writing this book is so that our children, the third generation, will see the big picture and not have all the problems we had. Otherwise, there is the danger of our culture eventually fading away. For example, my young granddaughter, who is an American citizen, doesn't understand anything about our culture, and so she doesn't understand us, even though she loves us.

When our children get married, some of my generation has problems communicating with a foreign son- or daughter-in-law. I thought this book would help them learn more about me and the challenges I have overcome. I want them to know that I'm happy about this journey—not because everything has been perfect, but because I've learned to adjust. To me, that's the key. You accept and learn. You look at the beauty instead of concentrating on the negative things.

Here's an example of a challenge I overcame: I wanted to have a Persian wedding for my daughter, so I told her, "Why don't *you* find a husband, since you won't let me find you one."

She said, "It will come when it's time."

"Well, I don't want to get too old," I replied. "I want to walk you down the aisle."

She just looked at me and said, "I'm not going to marry someone I don't love just so you can walk me down the aisle."

So I didn't get my wish. But she met and married a young man who I love so much. And though I never walked her down the aisle, that's not important anymore. When I see the love between them, that gives me so much satisfaction. I'm grateful to my son-in-law for bringing so much happiness to my daughter. I hope every parent of an Iranian-American who gets married—whether to another Iranian-American, or to someone from this or another culture—will feel the same. (And now, I don't have to worry anymore about what time my daughter is coming home, because someone else has taken over.)

It's important to me to express appreciation to everyone in my life— my daughter, my son, my son-in-law, my grandchildren, and more. To me, maturity means learning that I have my own life to live, and they have their own. I need to respect their rights, and I hope they will also give me the right-of-way in my life.

I'm glad that my children, the new generation, have learned to call America home. Their lifestyle has changed for the better, because they appreciate the blessings and opportunities they are enjoying, here. There is no way they want to go back and live in Iran. They may want to go for a visit, since they're proud to be Iranians, but they would rather be American-Iranians.

THE BIGGER PICTURE

I hope I have made it clear that, in my view, eventually no one who came from Iran to America—including the older generation, my generation, my children's generation, and now my grandchildren's generation—was a loser. I say this even though the outcome was not good for everyone. A lot of people lost everything they had, all their wealth, by coming here; and that was hard for them. And a lot of people didn't make it, here— emotionally, physically, or financially. I know a number of people who were really miserable because of all these changes.

But at the same time, I see that their children are so happy here that the parents are more than happy to have made the sacrifice, even if they lost everything in the process. So even the losers are really winners, because their sacrifice has brought their children such a good life. And the children respect and appreciate their parents for what they went through for them. After all, the whole migration is mostly for the future generation—the real winners.

And we are *all* "proud parents" of these new kids on the block—all the Iranian physicians and attorneys, all the powerful Iranian-Americans who have added so much to American culture: its science, architecture, arts, music, sports, business, and so on.

Here are a few examples:

- **Bijan Pakzad** was a designer of menswear, jewelry, and men's and women's fragrances. With his boutique on Rodeo Drive in Los Angeles, he dressed some of the world's most influential men, such as: U.S. presidents Barack Obama and Ronald Reagan; actors Sir Anthony Hopkins and Tom Cruise; and sports star Michael Jordan. His jewelry and fragrances have won many awards.

- **Pierre Omidyar** is a French-born Iranian-American entrepreneur and philanthropist, the founder and chairman of eBay, the online auction site. His Omidyar Network has invested $270 million in non-profit and for-profit businesses to help economic, social, and cultural change.

- **Andre Agassi** is a retired professional tennis player, former world number-one, and one of the game's most dominant players from the early 1990s to the mid-2000s. One of the most charismatic players in the history of the sport, Agassi won eight Grand Slam titles and an Olympic Gold Medal. He's the founder of Andre Agassi Charitable Foundation, which has raised over $60 million for at-risk children in southern Nevada. In 2001, the foundation opened the Andre Agassi College Prep Academy in Las Vegas, a K-12 public charter school for at-risk children.

- **Tony Petrossian** was an acclaimed director of commercials and music videos.
- **Christine Amanpour** is an award-winning broadcast journalist, the Chief International Correspondent for CNN and Global Affairs Anchor of ABC News. She has covered many of the most important political stories of the past few decades, such as the fall of communism, Hurricane Katrina, the Gulf and Balkan Wars, Rwanda, and the Iran-Iraq War. She has conducted exclusive interviews with Iranian presidents Mahmoud Ahmadinejad and Mohammed Khatsmi, and was the first international correspondent to interview English Prime Minister Tony Blair and French President Jacques Chirac.

In concluding, I would like to express my gratitude for the opportunity to be part of this country. And I'm sure our children are thankful to their parents for making the move. And our parents, I think, are thankful to us as well for helping them to adapt.

Altogether, the outcome of the transition was beautiful, in spite of all the pain and losses, because it brought a lot of happiness to the new generation. I, myself, have gone through a lot of heartaches; but when I look at the lives my children lead, it all feels worth it.

THE GOOD NEWS FOR AMERICANS (AND THEIR FAMILIES) WHO MARRY IRANIAN-AMERICANS

A woman sent an email to my KShar's Kitchen website: "My daughter is marrying an Iranian," she wrote, "and I was so scared. But when I went to your site, I realized how fortunate I am. And now I'm proud of having an Iranian as a son-in-law."

When people get to know Iranians on an individual basis, they are much more generous and forgiving. Marriages can come about. Both my son and my daughter married Americans. They had no problem with it. They saw it as a journey—the proper way to look at it.

For those people who walk into our lives and become part of them, may this book be an intimate guide to our culture, so they understand who we are, how we do things, and why. This will ease the way for Americans who marry into an Iranian family.

They will find that although Iranian-American children have adapted to this new culture, their roots still go deep. They keep some of the old customs, like the Persian wedding ceremony and Persian New Year. When mutual understanding between people of different cultures takes place, everything can thrive. So if you know what I am representing with my culture, and I know what you are representing with your culture, it's much easier. Then each of us has a choice about which part we want to accept, and which part we want to let go of. We understand that neither of us is here to take each other's culture away, but instead to be enriched by learning about another culture.

When you marry someone from a different culture, if you truly love them you realize that you're also marrying their community and cultural background. In Persian culture, as in any Middle-Eastern culture, the family is much tighter than in American culture; so you not only have to relate to your in-laws, but you also have to relate to your *in-laws'* in-laws. So the more flexible you are as a newcomer to Persian culture, the easier your life will be.

Once you have read this book all the way through, then when you walk into the life of a Persian person you will have a frame of reference, know what to expect and how to act, and thereby be happier in the relationship. You won't be scared, worrying about what you got yourself into. You won't have to become someone you're not, or to give up your own culture. Instead, you can gain more knowledge and understanding about your new surroundings, and the willingness to become a bigger person.

Meeting a Persian man or woman in America is different from their counterparts in Iran, because they have been exposed to a different culture.

It's much easier for an American man to get along with a Persian woman who was born here, rather than one who grew up in Iran. This makes it easier for my son-in-law (who was born in America but has a French background) and my daughter, who also is from here. And they both have parents who understand their situation. That's the important part. Once again, I come back to how crucial understanding is.

Chapter 4

FROM KAMRAN SHARAREH TO CHEF KSHAR

Turning the Near-Loss of Our Tradition into
a Nourishing, Culture-Restoring Mission

Despite the wins to come out of the move to the new country, I had to acknowledge my distress at the growing distance between the generations, especially mine and my children's.

Maybe it was like this for American-born parents with their grown children, too. Americans called it "the generation gap." But as a parent of children from the hyphenated new culture (Iranian-Americans). I felt it more keenly. For it was not only a generational gap that threatens to separate us: it was also a cultural gap.

This was not at all what I had in mind, all those years I was working to bridge the generations.

THE GENERATIONAL GAP AND THE CULTURAL GAP

This distance, as I saw it, was due to a combination of many things. For one, our children, having grown up in this country and absorbed its ways, were not communicating with us so much, any more. The world had changed a great deal in the past few decades—many of these, remarkable changes that we as their parents were lucky enough to witness—and our children did not seem to realize how much. For they had caught on to their American ways, and ridden them speedily down the highway, stopping to refuel and gauge their maps but not looking back. And we—well, we had tried to integrate the ways of the new culture, but we could never do it as readily as them.

The children of the hyphenated culture were sprinting off on their own, and leaving us behind. Unaware that their easy triumphs were baffling puzzles to us, they acted frustrated with us that we could not catch up in those areas that they had learned young enough to make part of themselves. I wanted to tell them, "Look, we are still trying to digest it all. We are trying to make sense of the instructions that came with our cell phones and learning to send email. We are getting older, and we cannot run as fast. You are already at the finish line, and we are still waiting for the starter pistol to go off."

I wanted to ask them, "Is that the 'Generation Gap,' or what? Is the problem our own tardiness, or your expectations of us? We want to support your life in this new country, and at the same time to feel close to you. We are willing to move forward, but you are outrunning us and we can't keep up!

"Whatever the reason, you are there and we are here. Is our love strong enough to fill the gap that is daily growing between us? We see you looking back at us—but do *you* see that we are getting further and further apart?

"But this is not your fault. You need to run fast. And we will do our best to stay in sight and hope that, even with the gap, we will still be able to stay in touch somehow."

Following Your Dream, At Any Age

Even with the pain of this gap, I realize that it's not only our children who need to follow their own dreams (and have us support them for as long as we can and be happy with their growth). *We ourselves* also need to try our best to grow, and allow ourselves to *achieve* (not follow) our own dreams. After all, we are seeking to achieve a goal, not just to dream. We need to make sure that we don't lose the sight of our destination. There is a different between dreamers and dream-*makers*. So go and "capture" your dream.

Don't say that we are too old to dream. Dreams make us feel a part of the society we live in. At any age, trying to be who you want to be is commendable. I applaud all who try to make a change, who respect themselves enough to take the first step to capture their dreams. Let's show our children, ourselves, and our generation that we are still dreammakers—that we will do anything we can to make a difference and give back to our community. We will not allow our age to stop us from moving forward, and yet the wisdom of our years will carry us through. We will make a positive difference.

I was fighting to be heard. And this is what I wrote. See: http://PersiaToTehrangeles.com/resources.

Don't say that the difference that we make must have a big impact. Don't worry about its impact. Just take the first step and hope that you will touch one heart, teach one lesson, and change one life. That is all we each need to do.

A Culture's Heart and the Generation Gap

So my dream began from feeling troubled.

I was concerned that if this generational divide kept up, soon our children—and then our grandchildren—would not know anything about their Iranian background. And that would be a terrible loss for them, as well as a difficult barrier for us. Our Iranian culture was starting to blend in with other cultures and was in danger of disappearing.

Cultures will always blend, and this is a good thing. But losing contact with your culture? For me, that is not an option.

So I kept asking myself: "How can I help to preserve my culture, and at the same time: (1) introduce it to those who are curious about it, (2) introduce it to those who are misinformed about it, and (3) teach other parents like myself how to get through this transition and improve our lives by learning to get along through these hard times?"

And do you know what I discovered?

Food!

If you ask the question, God gives you the answer. Because now I realized that my children loved to *eat* Persian food, but they did not know how to *cook* it. "Sushi is taking over *abghosht*!" I exclaimed. (*Abghosht* is a long-simmered lamb-and-vegetable stew.) And now that I saw this, I could not let it happen.

"What can I do?" I asked myself sincerely. "What is in my power to do that will turn this around?"

The answer did not come all at once, like a bolt of lightning. But slowly came the answer to a question I had been asking almost all my life. It was a profound and spiritual understanding.

Finding My Purpose

All my life, I have asked myself, "What is my mission? What am I here on earth to do?"

And "Who am I?" This question, especially, I would ask myself often—but always on my birthday. Every year on my birthday, February 20th, I would first write down the inner questions that burned in my soul, then write down the answers that came to me in response.

It was on February 20, 2009 that the answer to my question came:

"I am a creation of God
who is trying to be worthy of what he has been created for."

Stunned, I repeated aloud what I'd heard: "I am a creation of God who is trying to be worthy of what he has been created for."

Now, I'm not claiming to be able to communicate with God directly. But I do believe there is a part of God in me as well as in everyone He has created. I am not saying that I heard God, but I did *feel* the answer, and it came through my lips.

So now I had a role in life—a "job," a title, and a mission. That day, February 20, 2009, I felt as if a huge load had been taken off my shoulders. And so, right there and then, I wrote this note to my Creator:

"Yes, this is what I requested from the Creator Himself. Now that I have come to realize my mission in life, please put me on the path I need to be on. Give me enough love to share. Teach me what I need to learn, and how I need to care."

And that was my birth into a new world.

I told myself, "It's now or never. I have been asking for my mission all my life. What am I waiting for? I need to follow my dream.

"I know I am getting older, and I know it is going to be tough. But it's worth it. It's the only chance I've got, and I am not going to lose it. It is my time and it is my life.

"I am going to dedicate my life to showing who we are as Persians and where we have come from, at the same time that our children are showing us where we need to go. They are leading the way, and I will not let all the negative publicity about Iranians wash our culture off the face of the earth. Generations before me kept the culture alive, and I will do it too. I will make sure that my children know enough about their culture to carry this torch forward.

"This is my mission for now. I will grab it, do my best, leave it in God's hands, and be happy that I've done my part."

And that is how KShar's Kitchen was born.

To see my son's interview with me about this turning point, go to: http://PersiaToTehrangeles.com/resources.

KShar's Kitchen

Since I have always loved to cook, now I thought, "What better way to teach everyone about our beautiful, deep culture than by introducing Iranian cooking to the new generation?"

So I began, even though I didn't know all the details yet, and not everything was in place.

"How will you support this project?" people asked me when I started.

And I always answered, "When you do what you love…when you serve people and give what you have…and when you also are trying to make a difference—the rest will follow."

Only seven months after receiving my mission on my birthday, in September 2009 I opened the door to KShar's Kitchen to the public over the Internet, with my website, http://kshar.net.

Sure, there were a lot of challenges to deal with. Imagine someone like me from the "old school" having to learn how to work with computers, from scratch. Fortunately, I managed to do it. Since then, I have had the honor of serving so many people via the Internet. The site has received over a million visits from people all over the world—both Persian-born as well as from other countries—America, the UK, and many other places on the globe. What all these people want is to learn how to cook Persian food—and not only that, but also to learn more and more about the Persian culture. With God's help, my mission has been successful.

And now I want to give you the flavor of what people have gained from KShar's Kitchen. Here is a small sampling of comments sent to me by people all over the world:

———————

"Sobh be kheyr K Shar,

Love the food and love how you show it in videos. Would you please tell me how to prepare *khoreshe kangar*. I don't know what to use for *Kangar* I can't find it here. I am so glad that you are here because there are so many other recipes I need to ask you how to cook.

Thank you and keep up your fantastic work,

Adeleh"

"*Salam* KShar,

I was searching the net for *adas polo* and came across your video. I am since hooked on all your video and recipes. I am new to Iranian food but I have learnt to enjoy it very much since I my Iranian boyfriend introduced me to it.

Merci."

"*Salam* KShar,

I love your videos and how you explain the recipe step by step. I've learned a lot from your videos. I'm learning Persian cooking, since my husband is Persian. There is this food, I can't find the recipe anywhere, my husband really likes it, it's *kufteh birenji*, I hope I wrote that right. I'm wondering if you could make it sometimes. Thanks a lot. And maybe some dessert recipes.

Nada"

"Dear my friend,

Thank you for your great videos and your artistic fashion. I found lots of similarities with the inspiration you have to look to the world with my own. I'm a literature student and doing my PhD in England and love the poetry. I do also love cooking, which I have created a little citation in Facebook, which you can check. While I was watching your *Ash reshte*, I notice you also make your own *Kashk*. I do it as well but yet it doesn't taste similar with what I had in Tabriz. Normally I cook the thick dough with a pinch of salt. Could you please let me know if you have other type of method in doing so? Thank you again.

With best wishes
Mahrokh"

———————

"KShar,

I came across your videos by chance on you tube while searching for a *Khoresht Gheymeh* recipe. I was exposed to the Iranian culture in my 20s and experienced some wonderful Persian cooking. As I am now in my late 30s, my craving for some of those wonderful dishes has intensified. I am now starting to gather ingredients so I can make some of these dishes for my wife and family to try. I live in an area of the country that doesn't have any Middle Eastern stores for shopping. Do you have any suggestions for shopping for supplies online? I am gonna try *Khoresht Gheymeh* this weekend and *Khoresht Karafs* and *Ghormeh Sabzi* soon after. The one thing I really miss is *Torshi* (mixed vegetable). Do you have recipe for this or a video? Also *Mint Sharbat*. I love your presentations and overall love of the food that you make…it really comes thru in your videos.

CMN"

———————

"Fabulous website. I love Persian food and this looks a great place to improve my skills. In your video '*noon va panir*' you add herbs to the feta cheese and walnut mixture. What herbs are these? You must forgive but I am not Persian so I am not familiar with everything that you know.

Amanda"

"*Salam* kshar-jaan,

Having a Persian colleague, I've visited Iran last march for the first time. Overwhelmed by the friendliness of the open-minded Iranian people we learnt to love the Persian food. Back in Germany for now two days we try to keep alive the feeling by cooking Persian dishes—like your chicken *tahchin*. And it turned out to look and taste brilliant. My wife and I love to watch your videos—your gentle way of talking, the exact description of ingredients and preparing the food and your exquisite presentation—*kheili kheili mamnoon* for all of that. I write this over a glass of tea and some *gaz* we took with us from *Esfahan*). By the way: do you know how to make *gaz*? Is it possible to prepare this at home??

Shab bekheir,

Matthias"

Get a sample lesson: http://PersiaToTehrangeles.com/ resources.

And that's how this book came about! People often asked me the same questions on a daily basis, and so I found myself writing the same answers over and over again. That's when I decided to write this book. I know that by sharing love, I am sharing myself. The best way to achieve my goal of really living is to leave behind a worthy legacy for those lives I can touch—and to touch as many lives as I possibly can.

At the end of the day, the best way to tell you all who I am is to repeat:

"I am a proud creation of God
who is trying to be worthy of what my Creator has created for me."

Other Aspects of My Service

In addition to KShar's Kitchen, I also am founding an online school, the Persian Cooking Academy (www.persiancookingacademy.com), where anyone can learn Persian cooking through my online classes. Also, you can find DVDs and other products there.

And since I will do anything to serve my fellow human beings, I also have set up a nonprofit organization called "Live to Feed." My goal in founding this organization is to feed the hungry, including the children. This starts from giving what I have and what I can. When we do that, the rest will follow. Love is what motivates me in life, not money. Love is the center of the universe; the universe was built around love. So the more you give, the more you will have. Love is a never-ending resource. Give it while you can.

To live is to give. To live is to love. To live is to share. To live is to care.

When we become part of a community, we need to contribute in every way we can. I am proud of being an Iranian, and also proud of living in this country, which has given me and other Iranians the opportunity to be a productive part of the community. What I do is my way of paying back. It really does not matter if you pay it forward or pay it back, as long as you pay and do your part.

The Rewards of Following a Dream, and Going Forward

A lot has happened since 2009.

The most important thing is that at least a few more people know who we are as Iranians—who we *really* are.

Another thing is that I have grown so much. I am not sitting and letting life pass me by. I am making a difference, even to myself. In feeling productive, I am going somewhere.

And so I want to encourage all those of you who are reaching retirement age (or as they say, here, your "golden years") that it's now time to get up and say, "I will make a difference!" Together, let's give our grandchildren a reason to raise their heads high and say, "I am proud to be an Iranian."

Can we do that? Will you back me up by telling your children, "We brought you here so you can have the opportunity to grow and become a better person by your achievements"? Iran is counting on all of us to show our dedication and our willingness to remain part of the best of it, no matter where in the world we are.

Let the following Iranian-Americans who have made a difference motivate *us* to make a difference, to give what we have, and to share what we can to reach our best, regardless of what forms it may take. Look at these inspiring examples of Iranians in America:

- Omid Kordestani: former senior vice president of Google
- Salar Kamangar: CEO of You Tube, vice president of Google web application
- Ali Javan: physicist, inventor of the gas laser, Professor Emeritus of physics at MIT
- Homayoon Kazerooni: co-founder of Berkeley Bionics, inventor of HULC
- Firouz Naderi: director of Mars Project, NASA

These are just a few names out of the many Iranian-Americans who make us proud to call ourselves Iranian. So get up and do your part, whatever that may be. And do not forget who you are and where you came from:

- Do not let anyone tell us who we are—that Iranians are terrorists, for example. We have over 2500 years of history behind us.
- Do not let anyone say that we are done, as a culture. We are just beginning.
- Do not let anyone tell us that we cannot make it. We shall overcome.
- Do not believe in what you hear from outside. Believe in yourself, and move on.
- Do not fall apart. We need to mend all the broken pieces. We need to unite and be one.

In Conclusion

Now I am in a new stage of my life. Yes, I'm getting older, but I also feel I am getting younger, because I am following the new generation— the generation of young Iranian-Americans who have the knowledge and energy to put this ship on course and bring it safely to shore.

As I try to do my share, I honestly can say that my life has never been so meaningful. Between running KShar's Kitchen, the Persian cooking academy, and Live to Feed, and writing whenever I can, I am trying to show everyone that it is never too late to make a difference.

Post-Script

1. I would like to make a suggestion to you, my reader: If a time comes when you want something to happen, as I did in asking for my purpose in life, write up yourself a contract with yourself. Then sign it, date it, and put it where you can see it at least once a day. You will be amazed at how it will unfold and become real!

2. You too can learn to cook Persian food and learn about the Persian culture! To avail yourself of this rich global platform full of recipes, teaching videos, products, and much more, you can go to the KShar's Kitchen website, my many You Tube videos, and my Facebook page. All these sites can be found on: http//: PersiaToTehrangeles.com/resources.

Chapter 5

PERSIAN FOOD

THE IMPORTANCE OF FOOD IN PERSIAN CULTURE

Hospitality is what Persians are known for, and food is the center of it. The spices, sauces, and the way food is made are what differentiate one food from another.

Rice plays a central role in Persian food, much like potatoes do in American food, and pasta in Italian food. I remember how my grandfather would spend a good deal of time finding the best kind of rice. (In those days, men did the shopping and the woman of the house did the preparation and cooking.)

Since I was always interested in cooking, even at a young age, when I was a child I asked my grandfather, "What kind of rice is good?"

And he told me, "Rice needs to be white, long-grain, and thin, and it has to smell good. The ends of each grain should be pointed." He knew what he was talking about.

To find exactly the quality he was looking for, he would go from one market to another. When he found it, he would buy a lot and store it.

In those days, there were no refrigerators. Most houses had a room that they called *anbari*, something like a pantry, where they kept all the dried foods. It was cool, and normally in the basement of the house. They would store the rice and other such foods in that room for years.

Learn about different kinds of rice: http://www. kshar.net/products.

The houses also had an *abanbar*, a cool place under the house where people stored their water, as there was no public plumbing at the time. They would walk down twenty or so steps (called *pishir*) to get the water. Here, they also would keep fresh produce (it could stay fresh for few days) as well as canned goods.

When it came time to do canning, pickling (*torshi*), and making jam (*moraba*), the women would get together and spend days accomplishing this feat. (To find out how to make *torshi*, *moraba*, and other Persian foods, go to www.frompersiatotehrangeles.com.)

The men of the house would do the shopping from lists that the women would give them. Everything was made fresh. Every morning after breakfast, the women of the house would concentrate on what to fix for lunch and dinner. Then they would spend most of the day making these foods. In the good old days, *everything* was organic. There was no frozen food.

As kids, we were given a choice about what foods would be cooked. Every morning before we went off to school, we would put in our requests for lunch and dinner. This made us feel important, and we could not wait to come home to eat.

Bread was another important part of our meal. An adult from the household would run to the baker three times a day to get fresh bread for each meal. And of course there were different kinds of breads too. *Barbary* was mostly for breakfast.

To get a taste of how it was done in those days, watch my "*Sofreh*" DVD: http:// kshar.net/products/

Sangak, *lavash*, and *tofton* were other kinds that a household would buy, depending which baker was closest to you (each baker made a different kind of bread).

The Foods We Put Into Our Bodies

Back in the old days when I was a child, nobody would even *think* about which foods were good for you or bad for you. People talked about the effect of food on their bodies without really knowing what caused that effect. Fat was very important, in those days. *Rogane-kermanshahi* was a very expensive animal fat that only rich people used to cook with. It was all about having a lot of oil in your food, and nobody wanted to use healthier kinds of fat, such as vegetable oil or olive oil. Nowadays, of course, Iranians are becoming more aware of what they put into their bodies, and animal fat is no longer popular.

Most of us don't really know *how* to eat. We tend to treat food as just something we have to do on a daily basis. We don't take the time to really reflect about, "What *is* food?" But since food is one of the most important elements of Persian culture, as I have said, I believe this is worth doing.

Food nurtures our body, just as our thoughts nurture our mind. Our physical body grows automatically; it's our mental body that we need to nurture and make sure that it grows in harmony with our body. To put our awareness together with our eating, it helps to look into the logic behind food.

Most people don't know *why* they're eating what they eat. In years past, we would put anything into our bodies. When I was young, nobody told us what was good to eat and what was bad. Back then, people were not as cautious as now; then, they would eat whatever was within reach. Those who were poor would eat a lot of unhealthy food, because that was what was available. Those who were financially well-off could eat whatever they wanted (but that didn't mean it was always good for them).

In those days, people didn't have all foods available all the time. Foods were available only according to the season: strawberries were available in summertime. Nowadays, modern transportation enables us to have foods out of season. But to me, they don't taste the same as when they are fresh-picked during their natural season.

Some foods, sadly, are fading away. There were some foods I used to love when I was young that don't exist anymore. Like the "rosewater apple," so-called because it was so fragrant. Now, nobody grows it anymore.

Eventually, thanks to modern food-production and transportation, people could get pretty much any food they wanted. But this did not mean that they knew what was good or bad for them; what they should and should not eat. Inevitably, snacks and junk food came into the picture. But some of these migrated from countries in the western world. We did not have potato chips, in the beginning. We did not have sodas like Pepsi and Coke. All these came to Iran from the U.S. and abroad.

In addition, there are some foods that we are not allowed to eat in the Persian culture. For example, Muslims don't eat pork. (For more on foods and religious customs, such as *halal* and *haram*, see Chapter 9, "Religion.")

Nowadays, however, people have become more careful about what they put into their bodies. This is because they are respecting themselves more. My own daughter and son have restrictions on the junk food their children can eat. It is so rewarding to see the new generation being so aware about their diet. Eating right shows how much they respect themselves. In fact, nowadays the *new* generation is teaching the *older* generation the proper way to treat their bodies!

Eating As A Family—Three Meals Every Day

In Iran, you eat three times a day: breakfast, lunch, and dinner. The family has to gather together for every single meal (with the exception of lunch, in modern times). I don't remember ever eating by myself, at home. There was a time for dinner, and everybody was there.

Family members would have their breakfast early, and then the men would go to work. Everybody would come home for lunch and eat it together with the family. Then they would take a nap for an hour or two, do their afternoon prayers (*namaz*), then go back to work for a couple of hours before coming home for dinner.

I remember being ten years old and coming home for lunch from school. As I walked up the alley towards our home, I played a little game with myself. With the smell of food wafting through everyone's window, as I passed by each house I would guess what that family was having for lunch from the scent, alone. I always loved cooking—I started cooking when I was seven—so I could appreciate good food. Guessing what the food was by the sheer smell of it was the game I played on my way home for lunch.

Another sign of lunchtime was the sound of *Azan*—a religious prayer that was broadcast every day, at noon and at sunset, to remind everyone that it was time to pray. As it happened, this was also the time for lunch (at noon) and dinner (at sunset). In those days I was too young to pray, but I was certainly old enough to eat! So the time we would all get together for lunch or dinner, and talk about our day, was my happy time.

These days, how lunch is eaten has become more flexible in Iran. Facilities for eating lunch at work didn't exist until recently. Once that was the case, the custom of eating lunch at home became more flexible. After all, some of us had to work and weren't able to come home for lunch, so we would take our lunch along.

Imagine coming home for lunch in this country and taking a nap, then returning to work for a few hours! It's a very different lifestyle—to me, a better way than the one we have here, where we work for 12 hours straight and hardly think anything of it.

Making A Time For Eating

I do not believe in eat-and-run. I don't believe in eating while driving, or eating in the car. I recently saw a woman eating food in her car in a parking lot. Here, people eat whenever they get the chance. But I respect myself enough to keep a special time for eating. Yes, there is so much to do in this country and people are so busy; but still, it would be better to make a particular time to eat. We need to make it a point to block out time for everything we do. Every day, block out a time for eating. Once this becomes a habit, you will come to appreciate it.

In addition, we don't take the time to *feel* what we're eating, to *experience* what we put in our mouth. To me, you need to give eating time. You need to really taste the first bite you put in your mouth. You need to concentrate on what's in your mouth. The next time you take a bite of food, see if you can taste and identify the spices that have gone into what is in your mouth right now. If you do that, what you eat will nourish you, and you will enjoy it more. -

A Recipe For Living A Good Life

A person who eats well is a person who lives well. A person who eats well has learned to manage their life in a proper and appropriate way. They have discipline. They know what they are eating. They pay the same kind of attention to what they are eating as to what they want in life. So they live a better life and are happier. If you know what you want, do what is right, and take care of your body and your mind, you come to a better place.

For the right way to eat, see: http://PersiaToTehrangeles.com/ resources.

If I were to teach someone the secret of happiness, I would talk about food. I would ask them, "How do you eat?" Because that's the first thing you need to learn. You cannot be a happy person if you're overweight…if you're undernourished… if you don't know what you are putting in your mouth. A person who does not know what to put in their mouth is just existing. They're not really going through the journey of this life.

I speak from experience. I have always had a problem with my weight. As a child, I was viewed as never eating right—and now I am paying for it. This is why I encourage you to watch what you eat. I always say:

- Watch what you put *into* your mouth.
- Watch what comes *out* of your mouth.
- Watch what you put *into* your mind.
- Watch what comes *out* of your mind.

Follow Where the Food Goes

When you eat, follow where the food goes. Not only in your mouth, when you take a bite and chew it—follow it all the way down. And give it time. Follow what happens to the food when you swallow. When you learn to do this, you will really be nourished.

You can even follow the intake of the air you breathe, the passage of the water you drink. Give it the respect it deserves. When you breathe, follow where the air goes into your lungs. Most of us breathe and don't know what we are doing. If it were up to us, we would die, because we don't really take the time to breathe. That's why God did not put us in control of breathing—because He knew we could not manage that!

Knowing Food = Knowing Life

We have been eating all our lives, and yet we have not learned *how* we need to eat. People sometimes eat things they know are not good for them. Yes, sometimes we need to cheat a little; but then we need to get back on track right away, and not let that go.

The knowledge of food will lead you to the knowledge of life. Nourishment is the most important thing in life. This includes not only nourishment of the body, but also nourishment of the mind—your attitude, your relationship towards everything in your life. Every time I offered my father any new food to eat, he would always ask me, "What is it good for?" He would not eat a food I was offering unless I explained the benefits.

Food as Relationship

Every time I cook and teach cooking, I talk about *relationship*. This includes our relationship with food, and our relationship with other people. Our relationship with food reminds us of our relationships with people.

So it's important to understand what you're eating—not only what is on your plate, but what has gone into making what's in that bite: what spices, what herbs. To really taste it. And then swallow it. This gives you the enjoyment of what you eat. It takes half a day to cook a good meal—and then we eat it in half an hour. To me, this is not doing the meal justice. So don't be afraid to take your time when you eat. This is your time, so let the full experience happen. You will be more aware of what you eat. I think the reason we eat all this junk, why we just put anything into our mouth, is because we are not paying attention to what we eat.

Food brings people together and keeps them together. There is a relationship of togetherness that food brings about. We need to be aware of this relationship, and to work on it. That's why I talk about relationship when I cook and teach on my website. For example, the relationship between onions and the other foods they are cooked with: the transition of onions, when you fry them and they blend with the meat and everything else. I always use onions as one example of relationship. When you chop a raw onion, it smells bad and can make your eyes water; but when you cook it, it becomes sweet and so delicious.

That's what we can do for ourselves as human beings. We can learn to become like an onion from the stage where it starts—raw and bad-smelling—until the stage where it is cooked, and becomes sweet and delicious. *This is the whole purpose of our lives.*

The most important relationship we have is the one we have with ourselves. Most people neglect that. But it's essential, if you want to live in a community. Even if you live by yourself and say, "I don't want to be in a relationship, I just want to be by myself"—still, the relationship with yourself is something you have to learn. Your happiness depends on this, 100 percent. That's why I always say, *"Relationship makes life."* The most important ingredient in living a good life is having a good relationship—with yourself, and the people around you.

Even our eating, from one culture to another—from *abghousht* to sushi—from where the onion starts to where it ends—can help us develop this relationship with ourselves. *Abghousht* is something that comes from my culture, and our children love it; but they also love sushi. So when you live in a world that gets smaller every day, you need to be able to adjust to different things that this world has to offer, if you want to live a happy life.

Food And Culture

Food plays an important role in any culture. When you want to talk about a country's culture, you talk about its food. Food and culture are the two things that really represent any nation.

In our country, food is not only a big part of our culture; it's also part of our way to represent our culture to other communities. So if we wanted to talk about our culture, the first thing we would bring in would be our food. (I will show you what I mean. Just come to my KShar's Kitchen website, www.kshar.net. There, I talk not only about the food and the recipes but also about the popularity of our foods.) In Iran, we have a very popular food called *abghosht*—lamb boiled with beans and potatoes, a peasant food. It's the cheapest way to eat. In the old days, people who had no money would always make *abghosht*. Now, though, food is so expensive that it has become a "designer food." Meat is so expensive in contemporary Iran that only rich people eat *abghosht*.

I teach making *abghosht*, as well as other traditional Persian dishes, in my "*Sofreh*" DVD. You can order it through http://KShar.net/Products.

When you move from one culture to another, in the beginning you have to get used to the new culture's food more than anything else. Food is something you have to eat every day, whereas there are other parts of the culture you don't run into every day. So food is the first thing in a new culture where you ask yourself, "Am I going to like it?" When we came to this country, we had to adjust to the kinds of food available in America.

The Art Of Moderation

When we talk about eating right, we also have to talk about *moderation*. That's another habit we need to learn—one of the keys to happiness. If we learn the art of moderation, then we will not only know how to eat, but also what to eat, and how much.

Anything you have in life can be good—like food. But *too much* of anything is a bad thing. Even too much of a *good* thing is a bad thing. So moderation has to be taken into consideration and acted on.

When you have too much of something, you tend not to respect it. For example, when you have too much money, you don't know how to spend it. When you have too much good food, you don't know how to eat it. People who have not learned the art of moderation—who have too much of almost everything—have a tendency to become selfish, disrespectful, unappreciative, dissatisfied, uncooperative, and too confident. (You need to have confidence, of course, but having too *much* confidence will make you cocky and self-centered.)

Having too much of something is as bad as not having enough. For example, you need air to live, you need water to live. But too much air is bad for the lungs, and too much water will kill you.

So moderation is the key to a happy life. This is what you need to learn in life.

Study Your Eating Habits, Study Yourself

It isn't only about food: you need to study everything about yourself. Yet if you study your eating habits, you will learn so much about yourself that can translate into various areas of your life. Studying your eating habits will help you become familiar with the way your body reacts to different foods and to different actions. You will learn what to eat, how to eat, when to eat—and when to stop. For instance, you will learn the size of your stomach when you know how many bites it takes you to be full. Then you know how much to consume, and that will be your limit of eating—your limit in that part of your life.

It's the same with everything else. You can study your *anger*, for example, and learn at what point you will reach its height. Then you can learn to stop under that point. That will be the length to which you can drive your emotion. Then you will be in control.

Instead of trying so hard to control each other, we should start controlling ourselves—controlling what we eat, controlling what we think, and controlling our own feelings.

For instance, there's nothing wrong with being stingy, being jealous, and so on. Nobody's perfect; that's part of who we are. Most of our problem in life is that we try so hard not to be what the community tells us we shouldn't be—for example, we are told, "being stingy is bad." So if someone tells you that you're stingy, you get defensive and start to say, "No, I'm not."

But you can use the energy of trying to push that thought away, and instead ask yourself, "Okay, I'm stingy, but what can I do to overcome this?"

At the same time, everything is relative. Someone who *I* think is stingy may seem very generous to somebody *else*. So you cannot believe what people tell you. You have to believe in yourself. You have to know who you are.

So if I tell you, "You have an anger problem," don't get mad—go out and study yourself. See if you *need* some anger management. Just because I tell you who I think you are, that doesn't mean that's actually who you are. You are who you want to be.

And if you accept and appreciate that, and give all your energy to moving yourself to where you need to be, then over time you will find out *where* you are happier. If you start from the place of, say, anger, and you want to study, "What makes me reach the height of my anger?" then you can grow. Then you also have a choice about when to stop: "At what point do I not want to go any further?" If you don't study that, then you go all the way; and the next time, you go further and further.

So to bring this back to eating: maybe it takes you 10 bites to get full. But if you don't watch it, you eat 11 bites. The next time, you need 12 bites. Then the next time, you need 14 bites. And after a while you find yourself eating all the time. That equally true of anger or any other bad habit you may have. The thing to remember is that you are in command, and you can control it.

There *are* times when you don't have the chance to think about the things you do. There are times when you have to react quickly because of an action that happens. Let's say that a car stops right in front of you. You don't have time to think about it: you have to put on the brakes right away.

But if you *do* have the time to reflect on things, it's better to study yourself as a human being, whatever actions happen in life.

I was 31 years old when I realized how many different feelings a human being can experience. Up until then, I thought there were only three: sadness, anger, and happiness. But really, there are so many feelings involved. If you really want to see and study the feelings you have for everything that happens in your life and everything that has happened, you need to embrace those feelings and recognize what they are.

Returning to the subject of moderation: too much control is also a bad thing. You need to let yourself go once in a while. However, you need to pay attention to that, as well. A person might want to let himself go for one moment; but then it becomes two moments, then three, then four—and then it's out of control. This is what can happen when you are not paying attention. If you are aware of what is going on, you will have more power to control it.

One of my own bad habits used to be that I would interrupt people when they were talking to me. This went on for some time, until at some point I *noticed* that I was talking when they were talking. Once I was aware of having noticed it, I studied it. this was because I wanted to understand it.

Studying my habit of interrupting enabled me to find out the reason behind it. It was because I wanted to respond to what the other person was saying, but by the time he was done I would forget what I had wanted to say. That explained I was so forceful in putting forth what I wanted to say, by interrupting.

This showed me that I needed to be a good listener. I wasn't, at that time. I always wanted to talk. I always had an opinion. Finally, I realized that this didn't say much about me.

Now, I hold back. I sit back and don't talk. Sometimes I would find myself wanting to say something before the other person had finished speaking. At first I tried to memorize what I wanted to say so I could remember what it was and tell the speaker, afterwards. But then I couldn't pay full attention to what the speaker was saying. Eventually, what I decided was that any time I was involved in a serious conversation or meeting, I would have a pen and paper handy. Then if something came up that I wanted to say something about, I would just write it down. And this is what I do to this day.

Had I not studied myself, I would not have become aware of this. I would not have been able to overcome this situation. And that certainly would have affected my relationships (negatively).

This is why I find it so important to study myself: to learn from what I notice, and to find ways to control things that interfere with having good relationships.

The Persian Relationship With Food

In the Persian way of relating to food, food had to be prepared every morning. The woman of the house would get up and make breakfast, and then the family would eat it.

In this country, you can make meals ahead of time. Also, there are so many frozen foods you can buy. But there, we did not have that liberty. Every morning, after breakfast, the woman of the house (or perhaps a maid) would go to the shops, bring what she had bought home, and start cooking for lunch, and then, later, for dinner.

Breakfast

Every morning, before sunrise, the shops would open their doors to the public, so that people could go to *kaleh pazi* (something like a breakfast diner) and eat *kaleh pacheh* (lamb's head and feet) for breakfast. People would mostly get it to go. Friday was (and still is) our day-off of the week (like Sunday in America). It was my favorite breakfast. You ate this all year round.

To see what a traditional *kaleh pazi* looks like, see: http://PersiaToTehrangeles.com/resources.

Halim—wheat and turkey or beef, cooked together with sugar and honey (a complicated process that took hours)—is another popular breakfast, especially in winter time, when it feels like a comfort food.

Even today when you go to Iran, you cannot miss the shops that serve these two popular dishes for breakfast.

The other main breakfast was *naan-o-panier*. This is bread with feta cheese or jam and butter.

Soft-boiled eggs were also sometimes added to the breakfast table.

And there was always tea. Tea was one of the most important drinks every day of our lives. (See the tea ceremony in Chapter 2, "Persian Traditions, Ceremonies, and Non-Religious Ceremonies.")

This is just an example of how important food was in Persian culture—and still is.

Lunch

Since dinner is the most important meal of the day in Iran, lunch is something that you have between breakfast and dinner. After breakfast, everyone would go to work or school. Then, after the lady of the house (or the maid) had shopped, she would prepare some lunch around noon.

Rice is one of the main lunch ingredients—basmati rice. Usually, the woman of the house would fix some stew (*khoresht*) to go with the rice.

The most popular meats and fish were (in the following order): chicken, lamb, veal, and fish. Beef was not that popular, then; but nowadays, they also use beef.

Dinner

At dinner, the whole family gets together. They have a main meal and eat it, and go to bed a few hours later.

Popular Street-Snacks

Del o gholveh: I remember as a child in Iran that in the afternoon, out in the street, you could buy *gigar del o gholveh* (lamb's liver and heart). They would barbeque it and sell it to the public for afternoon snack.

To see *del o gholveh* on a street corner, go to: http://PersiaToTehrangeles.com/resources.

Ballal: Grilled corn also was sold on street corners. This was something like *del o gholveh*, which was grilled on street corners every summer afternoon. Especially on Friday afternoon, children and adults would come out in the streets and buy these snacks and eat them.

I teach how to make *Ballal* in the "*Kabab*" DVD: http://kshar.net/products.

Gerdo: Fresh walnut, when in season. It was amazing, in those days, to be able to walk up and down the street corners and see the sheer traffic—the number of people out to have a good time while getting something to eat.

Other Popular Dishes

Other popular Persian dishes include the following:

Bread: Among the traditional Iranian foods, there are some things that complement the table and have to be there. One is bread. A popular bread of Iran is *naan-sangak* (which is crispy, thinner). It's cooked in a *tanoor*—an oven made of clay, with pebbles at the bottom. The other is *naan taffton* (made with flour, not wheat). And there is also *naan barbari* (made with flour, thicker). Another kind is *lavosh*, which is thinner. (These last are cooked in a *tanoor* with metal at the bottom.)

Rice (*Polo*): The main popular food is rice (*polo*). Here are some kinds of polo dishes, generally the most popular:

- *Shirin-polo*. This is the main dish we use for weddings. It is rice with saffron, orange peel, carrots, sugar, and barberry (which is like a small cranberry). [To learn how to cook *shirin-polo*, see: http://kshar.net/shirin-polo/]
- *Tahchin* is another popular food. This is saffron rice with chicken. [To learn how to cook *tahchin*, see: http://kshar.net/tahchin-morgh-chicken-baked/]

- *Zereshk-polo*: barberry rice. [To learn how to cook this, see: http://kshar.net/zereshk-polo/]
- *Baghali-polo*—lima beans and rice with dill. [To learn how to cook this dish, see: http://kshar.net/how-to-cook-baghaly-polo/]
- *Albalo-polo*—sour-cherry rice. [To learn how to cook *albalo-polo*, see: http://kshar.net/how-to-cook-albaloo-polo-persian-sour-cherry-rice-videos/]
- *Lubia-polo*—green beans and rice. [To learn how to cook this delicious dish, see: http://kshar.net/lubia-polo-green-bean-and-rice/]

Other polo recipes that you can learn to cook on my website include:

- *Sabzi polo mahi* (rice with chopped herbs, served with fish). [http://kshar.net/sabzi-polo-mahi-kookoo-sabzi/]
- *Kalam polo* (rice with cabbage). [http://kshar.net/kalam-polo-videos/]
- *Adas polo* (rice with lentils). [http://kshar.net/adas-polo/]

Meat or beans: After rice comes the meat portion, or beans. As mentioned, the meat portion can include chicken, lamb, veal, and fish. (Beef was not popular in the old days, but is used more frequently now.)

Stews (*Khoreshte*): Popular stews include:
- *Ghormeh-sabzi*—vegetable stew. [To learn how to make this dish, see: http://kshar.net/ghormeh-sabzi/]
- *Bademjan*—eggplant stew. [To learn how to make *khorak-bademjan,* see: http://kshar.net/khorak-bademjan/]
- *Karafs*—celery stew. [To learn how to make *khoresht-karafs,* see: http://kshar.net/khoresht-karafs-celery-stew/]

Soups (*ash*): We also have all kinds of soups and *ashes* (*ash* is like a noodle soup with beans). We have chicken soup, barley soup, and many other soups. In winter, we mostly have stews and soups, because it gets very cold in Iran. In summer we sometimes have cold soups. [For the recipe and how-to video for *Ash-reshteh*—beans and noodle soup—see: http://kshar.net/ash-reshteh-tahcheen-how-to-videos/]

Fruits: All kinds of seasonal fruits are a big part of our life. Melons of all kinds are the most popular. There are also apples, strawberries, berries, dates, and more.

Fruit, in addition to supporting health, is an important part of Iranian hospitality. And Iranians are known for their hospitality. Every time you go into an Iranian house, the host always has a bowl of fruit to offer you—also tea and sweets. You always find something to eat. It's part of welcoming you. In fact, your hosts are offended if you don't eat anything.

Vegetables: Fresh vegetables are popular, such as tomatoes, celery, eggplant, onions, radishes, and more. As with fruit, everything that's available in an American supermarket that was grown in the U.S. is also available in Iran.

Learn how to make both traditional and KShar-style *noon o panier*: http://PersiaToTehrangeles.com/resources.

Herbs: There is always a tray of herbs and *panier* at the table—at lunch as well as at dinner. Dill weed is very popular in Iran, as well as tarragon, mint, cilantro, and other herbs.

Ajeel: Agil is a mixture of nuts and seeds that is served on the last Wednesday before the Persian New Year. This dish combines several different kinds of nuts, raisins, dried fruit, and roasted chickpeas. There is also another kind of *agil, agil moshgal-gosha*. Since *moshgal* means "problem," and *ghosha* means "open," what this means is that when you eat *agil moshgal-ghosha*, all your troubles will go away.

Syrup Water (*Sharbat*): Sharbat is the syrup-water made from different fruits. Different flavors of syrup are used for various occasions. For example, quince *sharbat* (*beh*) is used to make preserves, and the syrup taken from that is supposed to give strength. Sour cherry syrup is normally served for gatherings and parties. *Sekanjebin* is a vinegar-and-sugar *sharbat*, traditionally served in summer for refreshment. Lime *sharbat* is often served at events such as receptions.

AND TO LEAVE YOU WITH A GOOD TASTE…

There is a great wealth of delicious Persian food, and you can learn to make many of these dishes yourself. Simply go **KShar's Kitchen, http://www. kshar.net**, and I will show you how to make them in your own home.

Chapter 6

THE TRADITIONAL PERSIAN WEDDING

I was 21 years old when I made my first visit back to Iran after going to college in the U.S. for a few years. I had a dear great-aunt there, Maryam, whom I loved very much. Although she was much older than me, we were very close. So when she asked me if I had a girlfriend, and how did young men and women meet in the U.S., I gave her a rundown of the situation here.

That's when she started crying. And, opening up to me, this is what she said:

"I was 13," she said, "and did not know my right hand from my left. My parents told me about this nice family they had gotten to know recently, who had a son, Hussein, who was 19 years old. His parents were looking for a bride for him. 'His mother likes you,' my parents said, 'and his father talked to your dad, and we said yes. Next week they are coming here with Hossein to see you. We think this is a good chance for you to start your family.'

"I had no say in it. This was my life, and this was how I got married to someone whom I did not know anything about. I moved into his father's house, of course—he was too young to have his own house, and he was working for his father. Later on, he told me that he did not have much say about our marriage, either. At least, his parents had asked him if he liked my looks or not. Mine did not even ask me that, about him.

"I did not even know what marriage was. My parents just told me what I had to do on the night of my wedding, and I started crying. I did not want to leave my father's house. I did not know anything. I was still a child. I only knew that I wanted to play with my friends.

"Before I knew it, I had two kids and was pregnant with the third. Seven years into the marriage, I realized that there was nothing about this man that I liked, let alone loving him. But what could I do? I could not dream of even talking about divorce. Even when I followed him to his girlfriend's house and told my parents—thinking, '*That* should give them a reason to ask for my divorce'—they said, "No, go and make it work.' They said, "In the Persian culture, you go to your husband's house wearing a white wedding dress, and you go out wearing a white *kafan*" (the white cloth you are wrapped in when they bury you).

"That was the day I died, inside."

My great-aunt continued, "I had two kids and another in my belly, and nowhere to go and no choice. My only reason for not killing myself was that I was afraid my children would have no one to take care of them. What would their life be like with no mother? So I stuck it out.

"And now I am 70 years old, and have never experienced how it feels to be in the arms of a man I love. I have never experienced how it feels to have an opinion about anything. I did not live."

My great-aunt Maryam wept while she told me her life story. I, too, was crying for her, inside. Hard as it was to believe, that is the way it was. Not all arranged marriages ended like this, but a great many of them did. The couple stayed in the relationship because they had no other choice. For all the fuss that was made at a wedding, in those days, both the bride and the groom were only children.

The truth was very harsh and hard to bear.

Now I will tell you about the way these arranged marriages were celebrated. Yes, they called them "celebrations"—but celebrations of what? Of not respecting a human being's rights? Celebration of destroying someone's life? Celebration of ignoring a person's existence and risking their life?

In saying this, I am not intending to criticize anyone. I truly believe that all parents love their children. The parents simply did not know any better, in those days. I cannot blame them for being ignorant.

So this was what things were like in the older days. Now let's take a closer look at what the traditional Persian wedding process was like from beginning to end.

THE TRADITIONAL PERSIAN WEDDING PROCESS

The traditional Persian wedding was a lengthy and complex journey. Modern couples, free to marry as they wish, may have no idea of what it was like for their grandparents, even though the spirit and many details of these customs may still be alive for the their parents. So I'd like to share with you this rich ancient tradition. It's always good to learn more about one's cultural heritage, an important part of what has shaped you; and if a non-Persian marries into a Persian family, this familiarity can help illuminate and support your relationship. Although we may embrace new customs, some trace of the old customs still, whether we are conscious of it or not. Learning about each others' customs and culture helps us understand each other. This, in turn, leads to better relationships.

The traditional Persian wedding begins with matchmaking, progressing through various stages, culminating in the wedding itself, and—months or even up to a year or so later—in the wedding reception. It is a story of families as much as of the individual bride and groom.

Phase I: Matchmaking

In the old days, when a boy wanted to get married, he was usually in his late teens and still living with his parents. When he had a sense of what type of woman he wanted to marry, he would tell his mother—not his father. Children did not have the kind of relationship with their father, in those days, that would permit them to open up and discuss anything with him directly. Everything had to go through the mother. Then she would talk to the father on the son's behalf.

The boy might say, for example, that he wanted a wife who was tall or short, slim or full-bodied, a brunette or a blonde, with a light or a dark complexion, and so on—superficial qualities rather than deeper ones.

The girl, too, might want to get married, but (as my great-aunt Maryam's unfortunate example shows) not have the courage or the right to speak out about what she did and didn't want. Based on the parents' ideas of a suitable husband, the girl's mother would start spreading the word and looking for a matchmaker for her daughter. However, the girl had no say about her own preference. There was only her parents' expectation that she would be well taken care of financially, according to more or less the same financial status as her parents.

There is a Persian saying, *kabotar ba kabotar, baz ba baz konad ham jence ba ham jence parvaz*—meaning, "Pick your own kind." *Kabotar* means "peajen," so this saying means "a pigeon should fly with a pigeon, and an eagle should fly with an eagle." In other words, people were advised to choose mates from their own kind. But needless to say, the bride and groom of that age did not even know themselves enough, let alone make an effort to know one another.

Either family could call on a matchmaker, or a woman who was sometimes a close friend of the family, and was well known in the community. The matchmaker would try to match the two families, based on their having similar financial situations. This was the main criterion; the deeper personal qualities of the boy and girl were not taken into consideration. The matchmaker might be paid money, or at least a gift for her efforts. If this step led nowhere, the matchmaker kept on trying until she found someone who was a match.

Once she had picked out a likely partner for the bride or groom, she would arrange a gathering (*Khaste-gari*) and then bow out of the picture.

Phase 2: The Gathering (*Khaste-Gari*)

In this gathering, women from the groom's family—mainly the mother of the groom and his sister(s), and another close female relative—would go to the bride's house and inspect the bride's face and body. This was done in a very respectful way: the bride would come into the room with tea to greet the groom's family, thereby giving them a chance to look her up and down. If the groom's mother and sisters liked the bride's face and complexion, then a second gathering was set up for the groom to view the bride. Since the bride would be wearing a *chador*, or veil, the groom could see only a small portion of her face; but the mother-in-law's approval carried a lot of weight.

If the groom, too, approved of what he saw, then normally a visit to a public bath house would be arranged for the groom's mother and the bride, so that the potential mother-in-law could see if the girl's naked body was free of any scars and so on.

If the future mother-in-law felt that the girl was indeed a suitable physical match for her son—and the bride agreed—then the next stage, deal-making (*Bale-boran*) took place. However, if the bride did not like what she saw in the groom, she could say no, and another matchmaking search would ensue. (Of course, she could be influenced by her mother to change her decision. Remember that all decision-making came down from the father to the mother, and then down to the children.)

Phase 3: Deal-Making (*Bale-Boran*)

The next step was *Bale-boran*, or deal-making. In this phase, the elders of both families met to discuss what the dowry would be, how much (in terms of gifts, not money) the groom's family would give the bride, what kind of wedding it would be, who paid for what, the rings, jewelry, and so on. In their view, they were showing respect by going out of their way to impress the other's family with the material things that they would offer. These days, we are more in tune with our modern ways; but still we can respect this heritage and the way things were viewed and done then.

One of the main reasons for this bargaining was because the dowry was always in the form of money, gold, or something of that sort; and in the Muslim religion and custom, after the marriage, the groom had to give the dowry to his bride if she asked for it. The dowry was the groom's obligation to the bride after marriage, whether they were together or apart. This is why the groom's family would try to keep the cost down as much as possible—to make it easier to pay it. A further reason why the bride's family tried to keep the dowry high was to make it harder for groom to divorce the bride. The groom's family had the same reason for trying to keep the dowry low, in case the groom later thought that she was not the one for him.

The bargaining was often quite intense, because the groom's family wanted to pay as little as possible, and the bride's family wanted to get as much as they could. If the families couldn't come to an agreement, they left and the marriage would not happen. But if they managed to find common ground, they would set a date for the wedding ceremony. This was also part of the purpose of this gathering: to set the date for the next event.

Phase 4: The Threading Party (*Band-Andazi*)

Before the wedding ceremony took place came a stage called *band-andazi*—an afternoon party for women to gather at the bride's house to do "threading" (removing all the hair from the bride's face and eyebrows). A woman called the *band- an-daz* had the job of threading the *aroos* (*aroos* means "bride" in Farsi). She would be invited by the groom's family to come to the gathering at the bride's house to do the threading and put makeup on the bride. As a courtesy, she would also do this for the sisters and the mothers of the bride and groom. This would be the first time anyone would see the bride all made up; in the Muslim religion and culture, girls are not suppose to thread their eyebrows or wear makeup before they are married. At this ceremony, they were served sweets, fruit, tea, and *Sharbat* (syrup water).

Phase 5: Gathering To Bathe For The Wedding (*Hamoome-Arrosi*)

One to three days before the wedding ceremony, providing that the bride was not menstruating (she had to be clean), the families of the bride and groom would rent part or all of the public bath house for half a day. The bride would be with her female relatives on one day, and on a different day the groom and his male relatives and friends would go. Lunch would be served, and the family members would eat, chat, play music, and sing. Depending on the number of people present in the party, one or more female *dalucks* would bathe the bride's female relatives. A male *daluck* (or several) would do the same for the groom's male relatives.

Phase 6: The Wedding Ceremony (*Aghd-Konan*)

The wedding ceremony (*aghd-konan*) usually took place in the bride's house. If the house wasn't big enough, then the grandmother or another relative of the bride was happy to oblige by offering her house. Most often, the father of the bride picked up the tab for this event. The wealthier the bride's family, the more lavish the gathering would be.

Pictures of some traditional and modern weddings are available on http:// PersiaToTehrangeles.com/ resources.

An important part of the ceremony was called *Sofreh-aghd*. The bride and groom would sit next to the *sofreh*, a large ceremonial tapestry that was spread in the direction of *ghableh* (God's house). On the *sofreh* were a candelabra and a mirror. The bride, wearing a white chiffon or satin dress (the color signifying purity), sat in front of the mirror. The first thing the husband saw when he walked into the room was the bride in the mirror. Then, when he walked in front of her to sit next to her, she would see him in the mirror.

They had never seen each other until then.

Many things were placed on the *sofreh*. *Espend*, a tray of dried herbs and spices in various colors, was supposed to protect against witchcraft. On the tray were poppy seeds, salt, angelica, white rice, and frankincense (*kondor*), which was burned to drive away evil spirits.

There was also an assortment of sweets. A large piece of bread on a tray (*none sangak*) signified life and nourishment. A platter of fresh herbs and feta cheese (*none-o-painer*) ensured that the groom would not bring another wife into his life (*havoo*—the second wife). The bride and groom would each take a bite from the platter to keep the *havoo* away. A jar of rosewater (*golab*) was also placed on the *sofreh* and was sprayed all around the room to purify the air.

Near the *sofreh* was the holy book, the Qur'an. Fruits, sweets, and tea were available.

While the *mullah*, or cleric, officiated, a few close friends of the bride held a large embroidered piece of white silk over her head and rolled two large pieces of sugar (large as loaves of bread) together above the silk, so the bride's head would be protected. This ritual was meant to bring happiness and sweetness to the couple and their life together.

For *sofreh aghad* pictures, see: http:// PersiaToTehrangeles.com/ resources.

After this, one of the bride's friends sewed up a corner of the silk cloth, using seven different-colored threads, which represented sewing up the mother-in-law's tongue. The groom's mother was present in the room, and the ritual was not mean to disrespect her. She knew that she could do whatever she wanted.

At this point, the bride would be looking at the Qur'an (or another book, for the non-religious), and the *mullah* would be reciting the vows for the marriage contract.

The *mullah* would repeat the vows three times, before the bride— playing "hard to get"—finally said yes. Then everyone would howl and wail, calling out "*lili lili*," meaning "Hooray!" Then the groom and the bride exchanged rings.

After this, the members of each family would offer a gift (jewelry or gold pieces, depending on the family's wealth, and sometimes money) to the bride and groom. Normally, the bride received much more than the groom.

The bride and groom then left on their own, for a while. This was actually the first time they'd had the opportunity to converse and get to know one another. After a while, they would emerge from seclusion and greet the guests. Sometimes a dinner would be served, then; but this was optional.

After the wedding, the bridge and groom were legally married, but they were still living with their parents. They had not yet consummated the marriage.

The interval between the wedding ceremony and the wedding reception sometimes could take up to a year. This was partly because the bride had to bring the furniture and other household materials and goods (*jahiziyeh*) to the groom's household, where she would be living. During this time, the two families were getting together, and the bride and groom could see each other. In the meantime, the groom's family was getting a place ready for the bride to move in—a room or flat, depending on the financial situation of the groom's family.

When the bride would finally leave her father's house for the groom's house, her mother would throw a bowl of water over the threshold behind the departing couple. This represented enlightenment and happiness for the bride's new house. By throwing the water behind her, the mother meant, "Even though you're leaving my house, it's always yours to come back to."

Phase 7: The Wedding Reception (*Gashen-Arosi*)

The wedding reception (*Jashne-arossi*) happened months or up to a year after the wedding ceremony. The ceremony started at sunset, when the groom would go to the bride's house and bring her to the reception at his house. Car after car would be blowing their horns, in this way telling all the neighborhood the news.

The reception would usually be lavish, depending on the groom's family's wealth or how much they wanted to spend. There would be a big dinner, paid for by the groom's father, with sweets and fruits—no cake or alcohol. There also was music, and the celebration would last until the wee hours of the night. At the end of the ceremony, after all the guest were gone, the two fathers would join the hands of the bride and groom in the presence of the immediate family (*Dast-b-dast*). Then all the guests would leave except the mother of the bride, who would stay over all night.

After the bride and groom had consummated their marriage, the bride's mother would examine a piece of cloth stained with her daughter's blood in order to confirm to the mother of the groom that she had been a virgin. This was basically a formality, as the rules of the game—the bride had to be a virgin—were known by everyone. No man wanted to marry a non-virgin, unless she had been married before. In that case, the matchmaker would have made this situation known to the groom's family way in advance.

To see pictures of wedding receptions, see: http:// PersiaToTehrangeles.com/ resources.

Of course, this is the way it was done generations ago. These days, this is done much more respectfully, in that there is no longer an exchange of cloth or questions about virginity.

Phase 8: Opening The Gifts (*Pa-Tabhti*)

The next day after the wedding reception, in the afternoon, the next phase (*Pa-takhti*) took place, consisting mostly of women. They would open the gifts that had been given at the wedding reception. The bride was now considered a woman, since she had lost her virginity, proudly assuming her place among her peers.

UPDATING THIS FOR MODERN TIMES

Well, times have changed since a few generations ago. In the old days, there was no chance for a couple to get to know each other's inner qualities. No one asked, "Who are you? What do you want in life?" These days, we respect our children; we let them choose their own partners. But this is not to judge the old customs, because they were appropriate for that time.

Today, young people of Persian or any nationality looking to get married might still use a matchmaker or perhaps just engage the help of a friend to search out a suitable mate. But the children have more autonomy, now. They might still observe some of the traditional wedding customs, though adapted to modern times, and inner qualities are part of the equation. At these ceremonies now, there is usually alcohol as well as a band, singing, and dancing, unlike the more basic traditions of 100 years ago. I feel it's important for young people to be aware of their cultural heritage and to be able to select what still feels relevant to them in old customs—such as the richness and communal spirit of the traditional Persian marriage—while simultaneously adapting to the requirements of a different time. And it's equally important for partners and friends of Persians to know them better by finding out more about their cultural background.

The Persian Wedding In The Current Generation

Now that we've seen how it was done in the old days, let's take a look at the way it's done now. For the younger generation, the *sofreh* is often done as closely as possible to the way it was done by their ancestors, especially when both the bride and groom are Iranians. But if either the bride or groom is not Iranian, or if one partner is not a Muslim, then there might be significant changes in the ceremony. Nowadays, beauty and glamour might take precedence over religious ritual.

The bride and groom will be seated on stools, and their guests are seated on chairs placed behind the *sofreh*. Both bride and groom are present from the beginning of the ceremony, and make a lot of the decisions about how it will take place.

The days when parents chose their children's partners are, thankfully, gone. Today's brides and grooms are educated, mature, and self-aware, so they freely choose their own partners. These young people have the right to lead their lives however they choose. And we, as parents, should be there to support them, ready to lend a helping hand whenever it's needed.

I want to share with you an instructive experience of mine. When my son was in his late teens, I was starting to tell him what to do, just as my father had done with me. My son looked at me and said, "I will do anything you ask me, if you promise that *you* will be there to take the consequences."

His comment made me stop and reflect. In fact, it stayed on my mind for the next few days. Now, I thank him for it, because it made me a better father. It made me more cautious about volunteering ideas and suggestions.

I realized, there is no guarantee that my way is the best way, and so my son might end up having to suffer the consequences of my bad advice. We need to listen to our children more often; we might learn something.

Do's And Don'ts For Parents Of Marrying Children

I would like to point out some "do's" and "don'ts" for parents on the subject of the wedding. Getting married is an important and also stressful time in your child's life, so it's crucial that you are there to support them as best you can.

Don'ts

As the parent of the marrying couple:

1. Don't ask them to do what you did when *you* got married. You had your wedding. This wedding is theirs to enjoy. What was done then may not work today.

2. Don't guilt-trip them if they handle a situation different from the way you want them to. They have enough on their plate. Adding more stress will not help the matter. Instead, be more understanding.

3. Don't attach any conditions to your financial contribution, if you are throwing the wedding or helping with the costs. A gift is no gift when it comes with strings attached to it.

4. Don't expect your children to put you ahead of them by putting your wishes ahead of theirs. It is their day, their wedding. Stay in the background and be content

5. Don't bring up the problems you had with your in-laws, as a way of telling your children what to do—for example, telling them, "I had to do everything *my* parents wanted," which means you want your children do the same.

6. Don't criticize their actions, as they have enough to deal with. Support them and be there to lend a helping hand.

7. Don't disregard their feelings. Put yourself in their situation before you make a comment.

8. Don't have a long guest list, if the children are funding their own wedding, And make sure that those guests whom you invite will be respectful to the wedding couple about their choices.

9. Don't surprise the wedding couple with an unexpected speech. Run it by them first, and make sure it is OK with them. There may be a lot that you want to say, but they may not want to hear it (especially at the wedding). Respect that.

10. Don't force them to do something that they don't want to do, such as putting them in a situation where they have to confront their husband- or wife-to-be.

Do's

As the parent of the marrying couple:

1. Do your best to calm the marrying couple down when necessary, and always sympathize with them.

2. Do smile, even when you don't want to, because your children may be concerned that they're doing something you don't approve of.

3. Do support them in everything they want to do, and be very diplomatic if you have to voice any sort of disagreement.

4. Do select the words that come out of your mouth, because they have a large effect and can't be erased. Don't say something that you may regret for the rest of your life.

5. Do make sure, if you decide to ask them to do something, that it is doable.

Here are a few examples of supportive statements:

1. "I am so proud of the way you handle each situation."

2. "What can I do to help?"

3. "You two belong together."

4. "It is *your* day. Do the things you want."

A Few Things For The Bride And Groom To Keep In Mind

1. If you are expecting your parents to fund the wedding or help out with the costs, expect that they have a right to voice their opinions. An open pocket comes with an open mouth.

2. It is your day, and it is all about you. But remember, you wouldn't be here without them.

3. Respect them, if you want them to respect you.

4. If they make a suggestion that you don't like, try to meet them halfway and find a compromise.

5. Don't put your partner on the spot and force them to do something you wouldn't do, yourself.

6. Don't have a big wedding on borrowed money. Don't start your new life together with a big debt.

7. Don't invite too many guests, with the hope of receiving a lot of gifts. Each gift carries a truckload of expectations.

8. Listen to your in-laws' and parents' suggestions before making your decisions. It will help you in the long run.

You have chosen to start a relationship for life with someone you love. Remember that with this relationship comes a number of other relationships that your spouse-to-be already has. Watch where you are going, and make sure you are walking on solid ground.

How to Choose Your Partner

1. Don't choose your partner so he or she can take you where you want to go. Your partner has his or her own direction.

For my Video series about love, see: http:// PersiaToTehrangeles.com/ resources.

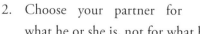

2. Choose your partner for what he or she is, not for what he or she is going to become.

3. Don't choose someone to complete you, but to complement you. You need to be complete in yourself.

4. You never marry one person: you marry a family. Make sure you like most of them.

5. If you are more attracted to your partner's wallet than heart, be prepared to live a loveless life.

6. If you are choosing a partner who is way ahead of you, make sure that you can run.

7. Don't choose a partner on the basis of what people say about him or her, but for what *you* see in him or her.

8. Don't marry someone in the hope that you can change them. Love them for who they are.

9. Treat your partner as the best thing that has happened in your life.

10. Do not stay in a relationship because you don't have another choice. Stay in it because it is your own and only choice.

Chapter 7

PERSIAN NEW YEAR

My mother is cleaning the house because *Norooz*, Persian New Year, is coming.

A child, I run to the door because I hear the man who comes only at this time of year, the *Haji Firooz*, outside in the street, singing *"Haji Firoozam man Sali yek rozam man."* This means, "I come once a year, and my name is Haji Firooz."

When I come outside and see everyone running around with a small jar filled with goldfish in water to put on the *Haft seen* (the special array of New Year's items assembled on a special cloth), I can smell the hyacinth and jasmine (*yas*) in the air. Apple trees are in bloom, birds are singing, and I feel as I am in heaven.

Then I hear my mother's voice calling me: "Come inside, come inside. We have to go get your suit from the tailor, we have to get ready, *Norooz* is coming." I rush inside. I can't wait to put on my new suit and shoes, to hold my parents' hands to go visit my grandparents, to see everyone with a big smile on their faces, hugging and kissing and telling one another *"Eyed shoma mobark,"* (happy new year).

I loved *Norooz* as a child, and I still love it today as an adult.

ABOUT PERSIAN NEW YEAR

Persian New Year (*Norooz*) is one of our most important celebrations. It begins on March 21st, the first day of spring in our first month of the year, *Farvardin*. According to the epic story of Persia, the *Shahnameh* (written by the poet Ferdousi between 977 and 1010 A.D.), King Jamshid originated this holiday. In the old days, it was celebrated because of the start of spring (the season of growth and flowering), right after winter (the season of dormancy).

Because many Iranians have moved away from their homeland and have been exposed to different cultures, many of their ceremonies have been influenced by these new cultures. But the Persian New Year ceremony has essentially been preserved as it has always been—and we try to keep it that way!

The celebration itself lasts two weeks, and is prepared for a month in advance with various ceremonies that lead up to it.

Norooz was not, in the old days—nor is it now—merely a celebration announcing the arrival of the new year. *Norooz* is an emotional event filled with love. It is part of our history, a celebration of time and of love—a celebration that only comes once a year for two weeks, but two weeks that nobody wants to see end. Children don't want to go back to school, men don't want to go back to work, and women don't want to go back to their everyday routine house work. The memories last a lifetime. All in all, this is a time that you have to experience in order to feel its many benefits and blessings.

I will do my best to give you a sense of it, here, so that you can celebrate it in your own surroundings and ways.

CEREMONIES LEADING UP TO THE NEW YEAR

New Year's doesn't just come on a certain night, out of nothing. There are various ceremonies that lead up to it—rituals that prepare you to actually let go of the old year and begin anew.

Cleaning The House (*Khaneh-Tekani*)

Khaneh-tekani is a ceremony in which you move everything out of the house and give the house a complete cleaning. It usually is done in the last month of the year, In this ritual, you throw out or donate whatever you don't need any more, such as clothing or household items. Afterwards, you bring back into your house those things you really love. Then you decorate your house and get it ready for the New Year. Why is this done? Because when you get rid of the things you don't want and clean and decorate your home in a more attractive way, you create more space for the things you really love. This helps you start the New Year with fresh energy and a new outlook on life.

Symbolically, this outward ceremony also enacts what you need to do with your *inner* "house," as well. We need to clean our inner self by getting rid of bad habits and bringing in good new ones. We all have our New Year's resolutions. For instance, this is a time to let go of thoughts that don't serve you anymore, and to turn your attention in a new direction. So if, during the previous year (or recent years), there was a sad moment in your life and you haven't been able to let go of it, now is the time to part with it. And just as with cleaning your outer house, here you can bring the thoughts that are dear to you closer to your heart. Then the thoughts you don't need any more will fade away or stay in the background. You still can bring them forward and give them attention when you need to, but because they will be back in the closet they will not have the chance to consume your thoughts and your time. This will give you more time to devote to new thoughts that will help your growth and vitality.

In the outward *khaneh-tekani*, the woman of the house starts the process, but it should also involve all the family members. The children start with their own room, which helps them gradually learn to do the same thing with their thoughts and feelings—the inner *khaneh-tekani*.

If you take your time and really get into the process of *khaneh-tekani*, each year it will become easier to do this with your inner self. It will help you start the New Year fresh, be open to new opportunities and new ways of doing things, and have a more flexible attitude. Don't get stuck in old habits. Make a shift, and be ready to follow through with the new direction. Encourage your children to do the same, to believe in themselves, and to trust their intuition. Don't put off for another day or month what you can do today. Some things achieve the best results when they are done today, not tomorrow.

I say this in hopes of motivating you to see things in a different light, and to move forward with your life. It's a new day. If your old ways didn't take you to your destination, find a new way. You are here to make a difference—so make it now, not tomorrow. Become the driving force in your life; take it where you want to go. You have only one life to live, and this is it. Don't lose this incredible chance to make it into the life you really want. The life you want to live depends on you, so take charge. Promise yourself that you will get to know yourself better this coming year, and that you will pay more attention to where you are and where you will be going in life.

Jumping Over The Fire (*Char-Shanbeh-Sory*)

On the last Wednesday before the New Year, a ceremony called *char-shanbeh-sory* takes place.

Several days before, a person called the *boteh-foroosh* would gather dried weeds (*boteh* means dried weed) and come to the neighborhoods to sell it. Each family would buy some in order to start a fire during *char-shanbeh-sory*.

On *char-shanbeh-sory*, the whole family would gather outside. Right at sunset, they would burn the dried weed and then jump over the fire. While they jumped, they would say to the fire, "*Zardi-man-az-to*" ("You take my yellowness") "*Sarkhi-to-az-man*" ("and give me your redness"). *Zardi* means "all our sickness and troubles—our 'yellowness.'" *Sarkhi* means "good health and good feelings, vivacity—redness." So all together, this phrase means, "Give me happiness and take away my sickness and sorrows."

Why "yellowness"? Because when you are sick or depressed, your face turns yellow and loses its glow. And when you feel happy and well, your skin turns red and you look healthy and beautiful. We have a Persian

saying: *"Range rokhsare neshan midahad az cere zamir."* This means that
the color of your face reveals exactly what's going on inside you—your
real feelings. What all this means is, "Health and happiness for the year
to come!"

On *char-shanbeh-sory*, you take account of all your aches and pains,
all your sadness and depressing thoughts. These are your *zardis*, which
you will be giving to the fire. In order to give them to the fire, you
need to know what they are. So take a day before *char-shanbeh-sory* and
go deep within. See what is bothering you, what is stopping you from
becoming who you really are and who you want to become, what is
clipping your wings. These are the *zardis* that you want to get rid of.
When you walk over the threshold of the New Year, you want to be free
of all the excess baggage.

Imagine that you are carrying a lot of bags, have arrived at your
destination in the airport. Your lover is coming towards you—but you
have to spend several minutes putting down all those bags. This is time
you could have spent in your lover's arms! Do you still want to carry all
those worthless thoughts and habits around that are keeping you from
embracing your loved ones, your life, your future?

People in Iran believe so strongly in *range rokhsare neshan midahad az
cer zami*—"health and happiness for the year to come"—that they want
to include their children in the New Year's blessing. So they hold their
children in their arms while jumping over the fire, to ensure that everyone
in the family receives the benefits of this ritual. Then, after everyone has
jumped over the fire, they come inside and celebrate with sweets: nuts,
raisins, dates, dried fruits, called *agil-char-shambeh-sory*. (*Agil* means a
bowl of nuts.)

A Persian "Halloween" (*Ghashogh-Zani*) Persian "Halloween"

What I loved most, as a child, was to go out with my uncle in the alley by
our house and take part in the ceremony called *ghashogh-zani*. Since I had
covered my head with a *chador* (veil), as was the custom, I believed that
nobody would recognize me: but alas, everybody knew everybody in the
neighborhood. Still, it was a great experience.

This custom of *ghashogh-zani*, which happens on the same night as *Char-shanbeh-sory*, is similar to Halloween in America. In this ritual, a mature man in the family gathers together all the boys who want to do *ghashogh-zani*. The boys throw a *chador* over their heads so nobody will see who they are, and then they go door-to-door through the neighborhood, banging a metal spoon (*ghashogh*) on a metal bowl and asking for a treat, which the neighbors usually give. Nowadays, this is not done as much as before, because neighborhoods are not as closely knit as they once were.

The philosophy behind this custom is that begging (which is so difficult for most people) helps you understand what it feels like to lose your pride. It teaches you to feel how those who are not as blessed as you are feel, and not to look down on them. It also helps you to appreciate more fully what you have and not take it for granted, because there are no guarantees in life: you could lose everything you have—your possessions, your health, your family. *Ghashogh-zani* helps you become more considerate and humble, because it is as if you are at *God's* doorstep, not your neighbor's. It is *God* from whom you are begging. In essence it is saying to God, "What I ask is Your generosity. And what I receive, I need to appreciate, as this is my share that has come from You." Behind this is the spiritual belief that this begging will teach you to rise to a higher level of humanity, and that in life we are begging for everything. Even our body begs for water and air.

A Persian "Santa Claus" (*Haji-Firoz*)

Remember my story about *haji-firoz* from the beginning of this chapter? Here is the place in the *Norooz* process where it comes in.

The last week of the month, after *char-shambeh-sory*, a man known as *Haji-firoz* comes as a symbol of the New Year. Similar to the western Santa Claus, he wears a red outfit. He also colors his face charcoal black, and runs around the neighborhood playing the tambourine and singing, "*Haji-firoz am man, Sali yek rozoo am man*"— "I am Amoo Norooz, I come once a year." While he sings, a man behind him plays the flute or some other instrument, and they collect money. They are sort of beggars, but in the spirit of the New Year. They are proud of what they are doing, bearing the gift of spring (*eyad norooz*).

The reason *Haji-firoz* colors his face black is to indicate that "My face is black, but look in my heart, which is bright." In other words, "Don't judge a book by its cover. Take the time to get to know each other. Get to know who I am before you pass judgment." It also shows us that everyone in society who is trying to make an honest living needs to be respected, no matter what end of the spectrum they are on. You are not to judge another person, because you are not walking in their shoes.

To see pictures of *hajji firooz*, go to: http://PersiaToTehrangeles.com/resources.

So you can see that these various customs are all related.

Bathing On New Year's Eve

Another important custom is bathing on New Year's Eve. Everyone used to go to the bath houses, since most people did not have their own bathing facilities. Like cleaning the house, this bathing was a process of cleansing not only on the outside but also on the inside. You wash your body because you need to be clean inside, as you are going to welcome the arrival of a new year, new thoughts, and a new you—a you who has not only grown one year older but who has developed a bigger heart: a heart that, in this coming year, can hold 365 times more love than last year.

Getting New Clothes For The New Year

Another custom is that everyone should have something new to wear for the New Year, so that you have new clothes when you go visit your extended family. Everyone has to have at least one new piece of clothing on their body.

The reason behind this is to show you to be open to new things that come your way. In fact, the whole process of the New Year is to show you that you need to open a new door, and close behind you the year that has gone and will never come back. It tells you to treasure today, for it is a new day. *Every* day of your life is a new day. So walk into it with the determination that you will make a difference and a change for better—not only in your own life, but also in the lives of those you love.

New Growth: Sprouting Wheat Or Lentils (*Sabzah*)

Sabzah is another part of the New Year. A couple of weeks before *Nooroz*, you soak wheat or lentils in water for a day or two. On the third day, as soon as you see that the outer shell is cracking and the plant shoot is emerging, you spread the wheat or lentils on a plate and cover it with a piece of wet cloth. After another two or three days, when you see the shoots getting green, you uncover the plate and let it sit in the sun so the shoots can grow. This ritual represents birth and transformation and growth. After all, we, too, all come from a seed. And not only do we grow physically, but as human beings we have the choice to grow in so many other ways, too. So let yourself grow to the highest capacity of your being.

The *Norooz* Cloth (*Sofreh*) Set With Special Things (*Sofreh-Haft-Seen*)

Sofreh means a piece of cloth that is spread out. Under ordinary circumstances, people usually will sit around it to have a family meal. At lunch time, family members put food on the *sofreh* and eat together.

But *Sofreh* is also used for other occasions, such as feasts, weddings, and *Norooz*. *Haft* is the number seven, and *seen* means something that starts with the letter "s." So connecting *sofreh* with *haft-seen* is a symbol of the New Year.

The wealthier the families are, the more elaborate their *sofreh*. Therefore, the more you have, the more you need to share with others. Every moment of our life is meant to be a moment of sharing.

What Is Placed on the *Sofreh Haft-Seen*

About a week before the New Year, usually all the family members spread the *sofreh haft-seen*. The kinds of things that people put on it include the holy book of their religion, candelabras, and a mirror to reflect the *sofreh*.

The mirror reflection represents what the family already had—the year that's gone. And the reality of the *sofreh* represents what's appearing right now. The reflection, called *aks*, is always the opposite of the true reflection. If I stand in front of a mirror, my right side appears as my left, and my left side appears as my right. So the reflection of the *sofreh* is *aks*. *Aks* also means "picture" in Farsi: the picture of an object represents the past of that object. So the message is: "The past is past. Look forward to

If you would like to create your own *haft-Seen*, check out the videos I have for you. http:// PersiaToTehrangeles.com/ resources.

the future." (To see what a *sofreh haft-seen* looks like, please go to http:// kshar.net/haft-seen-norouz/.)

Another reason for the mirror is that its surface is so smooth and bright that you can see your reflection in it. The symbolism of this is that you have to be as pure and clear as a mirror, so that this will be reflected in your face. Because your face is the mirror of how you are inside.

What does the *sofreh* mean?

Because the birth of the human spirit goes through seven stages (we call it the "seven heavens") and the number seven refers to the highest level of the human spirit, we have seven components in the *sofreh-haft-seen*, each representing something. And each of these foods or herbs starts with the letter "s":

1. *Seer*: garlic.

2. *Serkeh*: vinegar. Both garlic and vinegar play a significant role in the elimination of diseases. We also have a Persian saying that when you boil *seer* and *serkeh* together, the result should get rid of all that's unhealthy in the body. And when you boil the two together in the house, you cleanse the whole environment. When people are worrying about something, they say, "It's like vinegar and garlic are boiling inside." It means you're worried, and you're hoping that good will come of it.

3. *Seeb*: apple—a representation of health and happiness. It means you're hoping to have a fruitful year.

4. *Somagh:* sumac—the spice that comes from berries. Made in Iran, it represents blossoming and strength.

5. *Senjed*: oleaster. This is the fruit that comes from the *zotas* tree, and represents love. When you are under a *zotas* tree you will fall in love, and you will love yourself and be free of hate.

6. *Sonbol*: hyacinth. It has a magical fragrance, and comes from east of Iran. It represents rebirth.

7. *Sekkeh:* a coin. It represents wealth and fortune. It refers to wealth—inner well as outer.

The Beginning Of The New Year (*Sal-E-Tahvil*)

Sal-e-tahvil is the spring equinox—the exact moment when the sun is at its zenith over the equator and the earth passes through the equinox. This is the beginning of the New Year.

The whole family needs to be gathered around the *sofreh* then, to complete the family circle. When I was a kid, just before *sal-e-tahvil* my mother would call me, "Hurry up, you need to come to the *sofreh* before the New Year starts." That's why the *sofreh* is a representation of the circle.

The New Year could begin at 10 a.m. or in the evening. Seeing the moon on the first day of spring means "tomorrow is the new year." Everyone wants to be in their own house when it's announced.

If the New Year starts at night, everyone goes to sleep after *sal-e-tahvil.* Then the next morning, they will start visiting—going to one another's house and paying their respects. If the New Year starts in the day, they start visiting within an hour or so.

To find out all about *Norooz*, see the videos: http://PersiaToTehrangeles.com/resources.

Children visit their parents, then their grandparents, then their aunts and uncles. The older you are, the fewer places you have to go, because everyone is coming to you. This is a sign of respect. And throughout, everyone is telling each other, "*Eyada-shoma-mobarak*!"—Happy new year!

The First Day Of Spring (*Eyad-Norooz*)

Eayde Norouz is the first day of spring. Normally, it's March 21ˢᵗ, but it varies depending on the position of the moon. *Eyad* means "a happy occasion," so *eyad-Norooz* means that the New Year is a happy time.

Gift-Giving

Gift-giving is another important part of the New Year. Everyone exchanges gifts, but mainly the older people give gifts to the younger ones—usually, money. An older person in the family places different denominations of money in different pages of the Qur'an for all the younger people. When the elder hands you the holy book, you open it at random and read the first verse on the page. Since it's said that the gift of God goes with the spoken rule of God, then this is your guidance for the New Year. And the money you found there is seen as your portion for the New Year. You would never look to another page to see how much others got. You accepted whatever was in the page you turned to, as your share and your gift.

I remember how my mother and grandmother would put brand-new money inside the pages of the Qur'an. I was always happy with what I got, whether it was $1, $5, or $10. (Iranian money at that time was the *toman*, which is like the dollar.) The reason it was in the Qur'an was based on the idea that anything that comes from God is your share of the life ahead of you. It means, do not complain. The life that you have, and the year ahead, are gifts of God. Appreciate what is given to you, and share with others whatever you have that's worth sharing.

Visiting To Forgive (*Dido-Bazdid*) Until The 13ᵀʰ Day (*Sizdah-Badar*)

Another ritual is *dido-bazdid*—visiting each other to forgive and forget. This is carried on from the New Year to the 13th day, which is called *sizdah-badar* (*sizdah* means "13"). On this day, the *sofreh* is cleaned and wrapped up and put away.

Those who are superstitious call the 13ᵗʰ day the "day of evil." Nobody stays home. Everyone goes for a picnic. Special dishes are prepared for the occasion, such as *ash reshte* (a soup with onions, noodles, vegetable, and garlic), *bagali polo* (rice with lamb), or *tahchin* (chicken with saffron rice). Families go out somewhere out in the field with their lunches and say, "Let's get rid of this evil day and move onto the next day." Everything—stores and all the rest—is closed until the 14th day. Then people go back to work.

To learn how to make some of these foods, go to my website: http://kshar. net/sizdah-bedar/

Another thing that takes place on the 13th day is that all the girls and women who want to get married sit on the grass and say, "*Sale digar bache baghal khoneye shohar,*" which means, "Next year this time, I hope to be married with a child, in my husband's house."

Our Persian girls don't ask for much. They aim high: they want the whole thing—marriage, a baby—all in one year. Mostly, they are happy with what they get.

TRANSLATING THIS TO OUR OWN TIME AND PLACE

Since a new year brings the possibility of new ways, my whole purpose in telling you about these old customs is so that they can be adapted into new ways by the current generation. Becoming familiar with the old Persian-New-Year customs and blending them into the new surroundings calls for everyone's understanding. In this way, the outcome will be both respectful to tradition and able to be lived in the modern world.

Imagine someone who has come from the Iranian culture to this country, expecting people in this new society to celebrate *Norooz* as they were used to back home. Our children are going to school, associating with American friends, and living in a new society. So we, the parents, need to realize our children's situation. We cannot prohibit them from having a Christmas tree because we say, "We do not believe in Christmas." You cannot choose another country as your home and not give your kids the courtesy of respecting the culture they live in. By allowing my child to celebrate Christmas, I am not disrespecting where I *come* from. Instead, I am respecting where I am *going*. If I do not allow my children to respect their current surroundings, I am showing them that *I* do not respect the environment that I grew up with. You respect what *you* have been brought up with. Let your children do the same.

In a new environment, we hold on tight to our old ways because we are scared that we may lose the connection with our past. So by allowing my child to celebrate Christmas, I am showing him or her that I am secure about who I am and my connection with the past. I am teaching my child to be flexible, which is one key to happiness. I am putting myself in my children's position, because I know that if all their friends are celebrating Christmas, it won't be easy for them to say, "We don't celebrate Christmas" or "We don't believe in Christmas."

Allowing my kids to celebrate Christmas doesn't mean that I am ceasing to be a Muslim and becoming a Christian. It means that I am celebrating every day of my life. Christmas is *also* a day of my life. At school, American kids do not ask Iranian kids, "How was your *Norooz*?" because they don't know anything about it. But there may come a day when they'll come to our house at *Norooz* and join in the celebration.

Our customs play a strong role in revealing who we are. So the more we learn about each other, the bigger we will be. You can live in the equivalent of one room and celebrate one occasion, or you can live in the whole world and celebrate every day. The larger you get, the larger your reasons for living will be, and the larger your goals and achievements.

I'm not trying to say what is the right way or the wrong way. I'm merely making a suggestion for a different way of looking at things. By allowing your children to be who they are, you will plant the seed of a better life for them. You will give them the chance to think about where they want to go in life. But if you keep telling them what to do, they may never learn to make their own decisions. And life is all about making decisions.

So this is how we celebrate our New Year. I hope this account will motivate you to celebrate your own life with new hopes and a new perspective, and to find a new way of giving.

Chapter 8

PERSIAN ARTS

What is art? Who are the artists, and how do they create?

This is what I always wondered, even at a young age, whenever I saw a tile-setter or mirror-setter working endless hours every day for a very modest wage. These artists worked so hard to create even a square foot of their masterpiece. This kind of artisan was called *Gach-Bouri*. [*Mashdi* refers to a person who has traveled to Khorasan (Mashhad), where Amam-Reza (the great-great-grandchild of the Prophet Ali) is buried. People become *mashdi* when they finish their journey to Mashhad, similar to becoming *Hajji* after going to *Kaabeh* (God's house) when making the pilgrimage to Mecca (see Chapter 9, "Religion.")]

Watching the mirror-setter who was repairing the mirrored ceiling at my grandfather's house, I asked him, "*Mash hossien*"—(*Mash* is short for *Mashdi*)—"does not your hand get tired, reaching up to work on the ceiling all the time?"

He looked down at me and said, "My hands are above my head reaching for the Lord, to give Him thanks for blessing me with this talent. My hands are the tools of my trade. My trade is the reflection of my heart, and my canvas is the ceiling of your grandfather's house. And my reward is your recognition of my talent."

He said it all.

What I learned from *Mashdi hossien* was that the artist's talent is a gift from God, his way of presenting it is his way of counting his blessings, and his reward is the recognition he receives from the viewers of his craft.

When you go through the *bazar*, you will see artist after artist marketing their talent—their crafts for sale—in hopes of getting some money to survive another day so they can continue doing what they love doing.

To view some masterpieces of Persian architecture, see: http://PersiaToTehrangeles.com/resource.

Going through the *bazar* is a journey into the world of art—a journey inside the God- given talents of these people: jewelers, gold- and silver-workers, marquetry- (*khatam*) makers, and rug-makers. And the list goes on and on. Every time I have gone through the Iranian *bazar*, I have seen many people from other countries walking around, amazed and mesmerized as they watched these artisans create and put their heart into every piece of their creations.

So in this chapter, I bring to your attention to the most popular arts that Iran is known for, as well as the artists behind some of these works.

These are some of the principal art forms of Iran.

THE VISUAL ARTS

Marquetry (*Khatam*)

Khatam is a Persian form of marquetry, an art form made by decorating the surface of wooden articles (such as table tops, boxes, and so on) with geometrical shapes made of wood, bone, and metal. Metals used include gold, silver, brass, aluminum, and twisted wire. *Khatam kari* is the art of crafting a *Khatam*.

To design inlaid articles for *khatam* is an elaborate process. For each cubic centimeter of inlaid work, up to 250 pieces of metal, bone, ivory, and wood are laid side by side. *Khatam* was especially significant during the Safavid era in Iran (1501-1736), when highly skilled artists used it on doors, windows, mirror frames, Qur'an boxes, inlaid boxes, lanterns, pens and penholders, and ornamented shrines.

∽◯

To see pictures of *Khatam*, go to: http://PersiaToTehrangeles.com/resources.

∽◯

Even though *khatam* is one of the oldest handmade arts in Iran, it is still very popular. However, it is expensive. These pieces are collector's items and, like any other art, they appreciate in value over time.

Woodcarving

Another outstanding Iranian art, woodcarving also makes use of skilled design. Here, magnificent patterns, inlaid in wood, ivory, or bone, are created, with simple or protruding shapes. Mosques, palaces and ancient buildings in Iran exhibit important wood carvings. Some of the Iranian inlaid works are preserved in museums inside or outside Iran. Common images include rose leaves and drawings of birds and animals. Old latticed doors and windows, made by hand, Iran are famous.

The patterns and designs first are drawn on the wood. Then, slowly and carefully, the pattern comes to life through the skillful hands of the artists. Wood carving on tables and furniture is very well known.

Tabriz Silverwork

The Iranian city of Tabriz is known less for its silverwork than for its carpets, pottery, jewels, and precious stones. However, silverwork spread to Tabriz from Turkey around 1915, mainly among Christian craftsmen, and today many objects are made of silver. These include trays, candleholders, fruit dishes, cups, and other decorative objects.

Before this time, silver objects had been thought of as luxuries, because of their high prices. But attitudes have changed, and today more people are decorating their homes with silverwork, which also can be a valuable family asset. Tourists in Tabriz like to buy souvenirs made of silver; and many parents give silverwork to their children as gifts on religious and ceremonial occasions. Young married couples often begin their lives together with silver mirrors and candle-holders. And numerous elderly people buy silver watch chains and rings. Two advantages of silver objects are that they don't break, and they are easy to maintain and clean.

Today, young people are taking more interest in engaging in this ancient art. Many of them work with craftsmen in the tradition of old masters to learn the secrets of silverwork. Vocational centers and centers affiliated with handcraft industries have been set up in Iran to teach silverwork to young people, creating jobs and giving Iran's economy a boost.

Persian Carpets (*Farsh*)

The Persian carpet (*farsh*) is an essential part of Iranian art and culture. Carpet-weaving dates back over 2,500 years. And the Pazyryk carpet, discovered in the Altai Mountains of Siberia and which showed advanced weaving techniques, was dated by archeologists at 500 B.C.

Over 2,500 years ago, magnificent Persian carpets adorned the court of Cyrus the Great. By the 600 A.D., Persian carpets of wool or silk were common in court circles. The Taqdis throne was covered with thirty special carpets representing the days of the month, and four additional carpets representing the four seasons.

During the Islamic period in 800 A.D., Azerbaijan Province was one of the largest centers of carpet and rough-carpet weaving (*ziloo*) in Iran. Small carpets were used as prayer mats. Later, carpet weaving flourished during the Saljuq and Ilkhanate dynasties, and a mosque built in northwestern Iran was covered with beautiful Persian carpets. Sheep were especially bred to produce fine wool for weaving carpets. Dyeing centers were set up next to carpet-weaving looms.

The major traditional centers of carpet production in Iran were in Tabriz (1500-1550), Kashan (1525-1650), and Kerman (1600-1650). There was much variety among classical Persian carpets of the 16th and 17th centuries. Common motifs included scrolling vines, arabesques, cloud bands, medallions, and overlapping geometrical forms.

Although these days carpet production is mostly done by machine, traditional hand-woven carpets are still widely found. In 2005, Iran exported $250 million of hand-woven carpets; and today, the Iranian carpet industry employs nearly five million workers.

Carpet dealers have developed a classification for Persian carpets based on their design, type of fabric, and weaving technique. There are over 50 different types of Persian carpets and rugs.

Wool is the most commonly used material for carpets, but cotton is frequently used for the foundation of city and workshop carpets. A wide variety of types of wool are used for weaving. Sometimes, camel hair is used. Silk carpets date back to the 16th and 17th centuries (at least), but are less common than wool carpets, silk being more expensive and less durable. Silk carpets are frequently hung on the wall like tapestries.

Some basic designs of Persian rugs include: historic monuments and Islamic buildings; spiral patterns; tree patterns; European flower patterns; intertwined fish patterns; and geometric patterns. A single basic design may be used, or a pattern of repeating figures. When long-established local designs are used, weavers often work from memory. For more elaborate designs, the patterns are carefully drawn on graph paper. Designs have changed little, through centuries of weaving. Today, computers are used in the production of scale-drawings for the weavers. Such technology has come to be a great help; but there is no substitute for the direct transmission of the craft through the generations. When you go to the carpet mills, you still will see young children learning the craft from the older generation. The skill is handed down to them from a very young age.

Women are mostly the ones who do the carpet weaving. They spend days to years working on a masterpiece, depending on the size. In the very old days, people who were quite well off would order their rug and have to wait months to get it.

Normally, it's preferred that the craftsperson who starts the work sees it through to the end of the project. They say that if the carpet weaver is changed in the middle of the job, the real value of that rug will be reduced to a much lower level. That is why rug factories make sure that the workers do not start a new project until they finish the one they are working on. But sometimes, a famous craftsman who is working on a rug passes on, and someone else will have to be found to finish the job. At points like this, the supervisor makes sure to get someone to finish the project who is very close in terms of talent to the person originally working on the rug.

In addition, attention is paid to ensure that the color of the rug is the same throughout the whole carpet. Sometimes, when the carpet is almost done, the remainder of an exact color of wool has been used up. In that case, the workers dye the remaining wool to match—but sometimes it does not match exactly. Here is where you will notice a lighter or darker shade. This difference will lower the price of the rug drastically.

Pile rugs require a difficult and tedious weaving process. It may take a few months to several years, depending on the size of the rug. Looms are used for this kind of rug. The simplest loom is horizontal, which is ideal for nomadic people, as it's easy to transport. However, rugs produced on horizontal looms tend to be small and of inferior quality. Vertical looms are more comfortable to operate, and are more often found among city weavers, as they are harder to transport.

Two basic knots are used in most Persian carpets: the symmetrical Turkish knot (used in some Kurdish areas of Iran), and the asymmetrical Persian knot (used for finer rugs). The Turkish carpet is tied with a double-looping knot, while the Persian carpet has a single-looping knot.

To view pictures of some unique Persian Rugs, see: http://PersiaToTehrangeles.com/resources.

Flat-woven carpets are important for the identity and wealth of nomadic tribal people, and are often used as floor and wall coverings, horse saddles, storage bags, bedding, and cushion covers.

MUSIC

As a child, I was always surrounded by music. In my youth in Iran, there were men who would walk around each neighborhood and sell written songs, promoting them by singing them. These song-sellers were called *Tasnif Foroosh*. (*Tasnif* means "songs," and *Foroosh* means "to sell.") In my memory, I still can hear one of them singing *"Mara beboos, mara beboos"* ("Kiss me"), which was—and still is—one of the most popular lyrics that has been sung to date. This, and my father and uncle playing the violin, was my introduction to the world of music.

I am not the only Iranian who loves music and appreciates its importance in our culture, or any culture. There are so many talented artists whose works have left a huge impact on us all.

In this section, I will only have a chance to give you a brief summary of the rich history of Persian music.

Ancient Persian Music

Persian music of the ancient world is not very well known to us, but we do know that music played a significant role in religious affairs. And in the much-later Sassanid Empire (224-651 A.D.), music was important in the royal courts.

Various instruments were used, such as harps, lutes, flutes, and even bagpipes. Another important ancient Iranian instrument was the *tar*, a long-necked, five-stringed instrument. The *setar*, a three-stringed instrument (a member of the lute family) was played at ceremonies with the index finger of the right hand. The *setar* originated before the spread of Islam.

A system of modal music (a melody type based on which the performer improvises pieces) was developed by Barbad, a major court musician. Today's classical music has the same names as some of the modes of the ancient era, but we don't know if they sound the same, because there is no evidence of musical notation from the Sassanid period.

Classical Iranian Music

Today's traditional Persian music began to develop after the advent of Islam in Iran; and contemporary Persian classical music is directly linked to the music systems of the Safavid Dynasty (1501-1736). Under the later Ghajar Dynasty (1785-1925), the classical system was turned into its present form.

Iranian classical music relies on both improvisation and composition, and is based on a series of modal scales and tunes, which must be memorized. The traditional relationship between musical masters and apprentices declined in the 20th century, as music education moved to universities and conservatories.

Some of the earlier religious restrictions surrounding music were loosened by the Persian Constitutional Revolution (1906-1911). So pop and rock music began to become popular. Traditionalists were critical of this, fearing that traditional music was being cast aside. In 1968, Danush Safvat, Nur-Ali Boroumand, and Reza Ghotbi (the director of National Iranian Radio-Television) helped form the Center for Preservation and Propagation of Iranian Music to preserve traditional Persian music.

Persian symphonic music generally refers to pieces by Iranian composers, usually based on Persian fold and classical melodies and composed for Western ensembles and orchestras. The term "Persian symphonic music" can also mean pieces composed by non-Persian composers, such as Henry Cowell, based on Persian music.

The vocalist plays an essential role in Iranian classical music, deciding what mood to express and which modal system (*dastgah*) relates to that mood. There are twelve main modal systems in Persian art music. The vocalist frequently chooses the poems to be sung, as well. The singer is accompanied by at least one string or wind instrument, and sometimes by an ensemble. In some *tasnif* songs (the Persian equivalent of a ballad, composed in a slow meter), the musicians might sing several verses along with the singer.

The musicians and vocalist decide on which *dastgahs* and *gushehs* (365 basic melodies) to perform, depending on the occasion. Traditionally, music is performed while seated on finely decorated cushions and rugs, with lit candles.

Iranian classical music has functioned as a spiritual tool rather than a recreational activity. Compositions can vary from start to finish, alternating between contemplative pieces and athletic displays of musicianship called *tahrir*. Lyrics written by Sufi poets, such as Rumi and Hafiz, usually accompany the music.

Iranian Pop Music

The Iranian music industry prior to the early 1950s was dominated by classical singers. Then Vigen Derderian, known as "the king of jazz," ushered in a new musical era that coincided with the growth of a westernized middle class. By the 1970s, Persian pop music was extremely popular. It used indigenous instruments and forms, and added the electric guitar and other new elements.

Googoosh was and still is the most popular musician of this period. I remember her when she was only seven years old and working with her father, who promoted her at weddings and parties. Later, as an adult living in Iran after the revolution, she could not leave the country. For decades, she neither sang nor produced music, and her fans missed her. Finally, in about 1998 she came to the U.S., where she has been producing and singing music ever since. Her fans are delighted to be able to hear her beautiful voice again. Googoosh is one the highest-paid Iranian-born pop singers of our time.

In addition to Hayedeh, some other prominent figures of the Golden Age of Iranian Pop Music (1970-1979) included Hayedeh, Leila Forouhar, and Darius Eghbali. After the Islamic Revolution of 1979, pop music was banned by the government.

Hayedeh was another of the few singers who came to the U.S. after the revolution. She died suddenly, and her fans including, myself, still enjoy listening to her recordings. Her death was a great loss to the music community at large, as well as to the Iranian community.

Like Hayedeh and Googoosh, many other Iranians fled to the United States and other countries, and numerous pop artists continued to sing in exile. Popular TV and radio channels and websites (aired through satellites) played an important role in promoting Iranian pop music and connecting the artists to Iranians all over the world.

In the 1980s and 1990s, a number of Iranian pop stars began to become famous. Many of them had lived all or most of their lives outside Iran, mainly in Los Angeles. This new wave of Persian pop music often combined elements of American music and culture, as well as Latino culture, to form a new blend of pop music. Techno music was also a strong influence. Some major artists included Shahrzad Sepanlou, Jamshid, and Shohreh Solati.

In Iran, pop music is subject to strict regulation. A permit from the Iranian Ministry of Culture and Islamic Guidance (*Ershaad*) is required in order to perform or publish music. There is a three-year waiting period to get a permit for each new album. Still, as a result of eased restrictions under President Khatami, in the late 1990s a number of contemporary Iranian pop singers have emerged in Iran, such as Sirvan Khossair, Farzad Farzin, and Reza Sadeghi.

Iranian Rock Music

This is a form of rock music that is largely produced, today, in Europe and Tehran's underground circles. It had its beginnings in Iran in the 1970s, influenced by traditional Iranian music and popular American rock bands such as Pink Floyd and The Doors. In 1979, Ayatollah Khomeini banned rock music in Iran. During the late 1990s, under President Mohammad Khatami, there was a more open cultural atmosphere, and underground rock and heavy-metal music began to blossom in the country. Some bands started using the poetry of Hafiz and Rumi on top of classical tunes and melodies, mixed with traditional Persian music. Currently, the Ministry of Culture must approve of the lyrics before a band is allowed to perform in concert.

Iranian Folk Music

The rural people of Iran possess dozens of instruments, but three types are common to all parts of the country: *Sorna-Zorna*, a kind of shawm (double-reed instrument); various kinds of flutes (*ney*); and the *Dohol*, a double-headed drum. Iran is home to several ethnic groups, including Kurdish, Armenian, and Baluchi people.

The most famous personalities in Iranian folk music are Pari Zangeneh and Sima Bina. Bina is one of the renowned traditional Persian singers. For years, she has been compiling a traditional repertoire of songs from the province of Khorasan. She sings in Persian, Turkish, and Kurdish, and sustains a tradition of nostalgic folk music that praises nature and love. Bahman Alaeddin (1940-2006) was a renowned musician, vocalist, and songwriter who made over 50 albums and composed many memorable songs.

Iranian folk music has been used by European composers as a primary source for their work.

PERSIAN LITERATURE

Iran has a long, rich literary history in both poetry and prose. Here are some of the major figures of the ancient and modern eras.

Poets From The Ancient Era

Omar Khayyam

Omar Khayyam (1048-1131) was a Persian "Renaissance man": a philosopher, mathematician, astronomer, and poet. He wrote an important treatise on algebra, and contributed to calendar reform. He is best-known in the West through Edward Fitzgerald's celebrated translation and adaptation of Kahayyam's quatrains in *The Rubiyat of Omar Khayyam*. Although Fitzgerald's translation has led many readers to view Khayyam as a wine-loving hedonist, some scholars view his poetry as having a much deeper spiritual meaning, based on Sufi teachings. In fact, Khayyam wrote a treatise praising God, *The Splendid Sermon*.

Shams Tabrizi

Shams Tabrizi (1185-1248) received his education in Tabriz and was a disciple of Baba Kamal al-Din Jumdi. Before his famous meeting with Rumi, Shams apparently wandered from place to place weaving baskets and selling girdles for a living.

He met Rumi in Konya in 1244, and Rumi became his disciple. Rumi dedicated much of his own poetry to Shams as a sign of love for his friend and master, after he passed. In Rumi's poetry, Shams (which means "sun" in Persian) becomes a symbol of God's love for humanity.

The *Maqalat-e Shams-e Tabrizi* (*Discourse of Shams-e Tabrizi*) is a Persian prose book written by Shams. It has a mystical interpretation of Islam, and contains spiritual advice. Here are some excerpts:

- "A good man complains of no one; he does not look to faults."
- "Joy is like pure, clear water; wherever it flows, wondrous blossoms grow. Sorrow is like a black flood; wherever it flows, it wilts the blossoms."

A large number of mystical poems have been attributed to Shams, although there has been some controversy concerning the actual author.

Jalal-ad-Din Rumi

Jalal ad-Din Muhammed Rumi (1207-1273), known to the English-speaking world as Rumi, was a Persian Muslim poet, jurist, theologian, and Sufi mystic whose powerful spiritual legacy has transcended ethnic and national borders. His meeting with the dervish Shams-e-Tabrizi in 1244 completely changed Rumi's life, transforming him from an accomplished teach and jurist into a mystic.

The founder of the Mevlevi Sufi Order, Rumi advocated unlimited tolerance, positive reasoning, goodness, charity, and awareness through love. He saw all religions as expressing a fundamental truth, and his tolerant teaching has appealed to people of all faiths. His main contribution is the concept of *tauhid,* union with his Beloved from whom he had been cut off, and his longing to restore the connection.

I recite poems of Rumi
and Hafez for you
in this video. http://
PersiaToTehrangeles.com/
resources.

His major poetic work, *The Masnavi*, a six-volume poem, weaves together fables, scenes from everyday life, Qur'anic revelations, and metaphysics into a vast, intricate tapestry. It is viewed by most Sufis as the "Persian-language Qur'an." Rumi's other major poetic work is *The Works of Shams of Tabriz*, named in honor of his master.

Rumi believed passionately in the use of music, poetry, and dance as a path for reaching God. For him, music helped devotees to focus their whole being on the Divine, leading to a spiritual awakening. It was from these ideas that the practice of Whirling Dervishes developed into a ritual form.

Hafez

Khawaja Shamsu Din Muhammed Hafez e Sharazi (1315 or 1317 to 1389 or 1390) is widely known by his pen-name, Hafez (or Hafiz). He was an Iranian Sufi poet whose collected works are found in the homes of many people in Iran and Afghanistan, as well as elsewhere. People in Iran today often learn Hafez's poems by heart and use them as proverbs and sayings. He has influenced post-14th-century Persian writing more than any other author, and has left a mark on such Western writers as Thoreau, Goethe, and Emerson. Translations of Hafez's poems exist in all major languages.

Hafez's book, *Divan Hafez*, is very popular among both young and old. This book also is used for fortune-telling, which is called *Fale Hafez*. In this practice, you make a wish and then open his book of poetry, or *Divan*, and read what is on that page. The particular poem you turn to tells you the answer to the wish that you have made.

Like Rumi, Hafez used *ghazals* (rhyming couplets and a refrain, each line sharing the same meter). The form originated in 6th-century Arabic verse. Hafez's *ghazals* expressed the central themes of love and separation.

His influence in the lives of Iranians can be found in public readings of his poetry and the frequent use of his poems in Persian traditional music, visual art, and calligraphy.

Poets From The Modern Era

Ali Akbar Dekhoda

Dekhoda (1879-1956) was a prominent Iranian linguist and author of the most extensive dictionary of the Persian language ever published. He also published *Amsal o Heham* (*Proverbs and Mottos*), and wrote a satirical political column called *Charand Parand* ("Nonsense or Fiddle Faddle") for the newspaper, *Journal of Soor Essafeel*. He was a key figure in the Constitutional Revolution of Iran of 1906-1911 that deposed Mohammad Ali Shah.

Iraj Mirza

Prince Iraj Mirza (titled Jalal-al-Mamalek) (1874-1926), son of Prince Gholam Hossein Mirza, was a famous Iranian poet. He is considered the first Iranian master of colloquial poetry, often using the words of everyday speech in his poems. His simple poetic language is also famous for its wit and satire directed at dishonest clergy, businessmen, merchants, and politicians. He also composed elegies for various Iranian historical figures, as well as poems on the raising and education of children, maternal affection, love, and romance.

Iraj Mirza was a strong advocate of women's rights, and compared the status of Iranian women in his time to the Dark Ages. Although he kept to the rules of classical poetry, he was also a leading innovator of Persian poetry.

Sohrab Sepheri

Sohrab Sepehri (1928-1980) was a notable poet and modernist painter. He is considered one of the five most famous modern Iranian poets practicing "New Poetry" (poetry without meter or rhyme). His poetry is very humane and concerned with human values. He loved nature and wrote about itfrequently. Well-versed in Buddhism, he blended Eastern and Western ideas, creating a unique kind of poetry in the history of Persian literature.

Ahmad Shamlou

A Persian poet, writer, and journalist, Ahmad Shamlou (1925-2000) may be the most influential poet of modern Iran. His poetry is complex yet his imagery is simple—traditional imagery familiar to Iranians through the works of Persian masters like Hafez and Omar Khayyam. Shamlou was an innovator, mixing the concrete and the abstract in a way unprecedented in Persian poetry. Quite versatile, he wrote plays, fiction, screenplays, children's books, journalism, and a 13-volume work on Iranian folklore and language.

Sadegh Hedayat

Sadegh Hedayat (1903-1951) was Iran's foremost modern fiction writer. Studying Western literature deeply, he was influenced by Rilke, Chekhov, Poe, Kafka, and de Maupassant. Hedayat published short stories, novels, plays, a travelogue, satires, literary criticism, studies in Persian folklore, and translations. He is credited with having brought Persian language and literature into the mainstream of international contemporary writing.

Late in life, he focused on attacking the monarchy and clergy, whom he blamed for Iran's repressive conditions. His most enduring work, *The Blind Owl*, has been called one of the most important literary works in the Persian language.

Simin Behbahani

Behbahani (born 1927) is Iran's national poet, twice nominated for the Nobel Prize in literature. A poetic innovator, she has brought to her poetry theatrical subjects, and daily events and conversations, using the *ghazal* style. She has expanded the range of traditional Persian verse forms, and produced some of the most significant Persian literature of the 20th century.

Simin Daneshvar

Simin Daneshvar (1921-2012) was an Iranian academic, novelist, fiction writer, and translator. She was regarded as the first major Iranian woman novelist. In 1948, her collection of short stories was the first to be published authored by an Iranian woman. Her novel, *A Persian Requiem*, published in 1969, also a first by an Iranian woman author, became a bestseller.

Forugh Farrokhzad

Forugh Farrokhzad (1935-1967) was an Iranian poet and film director, one of Iran's most influential female poets of the 20th century. She was a controversial modernist poet, and an iconoclast. As a female divorcee writing poetry with a strong feminine voice, she became the focus of much negative attention. Her poetry was banned for over a decade after the Islamic Revolution. After her untimely death in a car accident at age 32, her poem "Let Us Believe in the Beginning of the Cold Season" was published posthumously, and was considered by some as the best-structured modern poem in Persian. She also made a documentary file about Iranians affected by leprosy, "The House Is Black," which won several international awards.

PERSIAN LANDMARKS

Iranians have put a lot of love and time into creating a great many masterpieces, over time. So many talented workers have been involved— including mirror workers, tile setters, designers, and others, all of whom worked day in and day out to create them. Due to lack of space, here, I will only cover a few of them in this section. (Keep in mind that the following landmarks are by no means the only ones, or even necessarily the best ones.)

Here are some central Iranian landmarks built by Nasser-al-Din Shah.

Hall Of Brilliance (*Tallar-e-Berelian*)

Tallar-e-Berelian was named the "Hall of Brilliance" because it is adorned by brilliant mirror-work and chandeliers of Iranian artists. This hall replaced another called *Tahar Bolour* ("Crystal Hall") built by Fath Ali Shah. It was eroded by dampness.

Image Of The World Square (*Naqsh-E Jahan* Square)

Formerly known as "Shah Square," *Naqsh-e Jahan* Square is situated at the center of Isfahan city. Built between 1598 and 1629, it is now an important historical site, surrounded by buildings from the Safavid era (1501-1736) such as the Shah Mosque, Ali Qapu Palace, Sheikh Lotf Allah Mosque, and the Isfahan Grand Bazaar. Today, *Namaz-e Jomeh* (the Muslim Friday prayer) is held in the Shah Mosque.

During the day, much of the square was occupied by the tents and stalls of tradesmen. There were entertainers and actors. At the entrance to the Imperial Bazaar, there were coffeehouses where people could relax over a cup of coffee and a water pipe. At dusk, the tradesmen would leave, to be replaced by dervishes, jugglers, puppet players, and so on.

Public ceremonies such as *Norooz* were held there. Also polo, the national Persian sport, was played there, entertaining the Shah and the shoppers.

The Maidan—The Royal Square

The Maidan was the creation of Shah Albas (1586-1628), and is a key landmark of Isfahan. The square was built as a two-story row of shops, flanked by glorious architecture—a bustling area of entertainment and business, frequented by people from around the world. Isfahan was a vital stop along the Silk Road, so goods from many different countries found their way into the hands of local merchants.

Masjed-E Shah –The Pinnacle Of Safavid Architechture

The pinnacle of *Naqhs-e Jahn* Square was the *Masjed-e Shah*, which replaced the older Jomeh Mosque for conducting Friday prayers. The Shah Mosque was built by Shaykh Bahai to display a vision of grandeur, having the largest dome in the city and being surrounded by a religious school and a winter mosque.

The *Lotfollah* Mosque—The Private Room Of The Shah's Harem

On the edge of *Naqsh-e Jahn* Square and opposite the palace, the *Lotfollah* Mosque was supposed to be a private mosque of the royal court—unlike the

Shah Mosque, which was meant for the public. So the *Lotfollah* Mosque was smaller, and lacking minarets. At the time it was built, few Westerners paid any attention to it. Centuries later, when the doors were open to the public, ordinary people could admire the effort the Shah had put into making it a sacred place for the women of his harem, as well as its exquisite tile work.

For pictures of timeless landmarks in Iran, see: http://PersiaToTehrangeles.com/resources.

Ali Qapu Palace—The Exalted Royal Threshold

This was a pavilion that marked the entrance to the vast royal residential quarter of the Isfahan city of the Safavid era. It was here that Shah Albas entertained noble visitors and foreign ambassadors. The palace, a large rectangular structure, had been the site of royal receptions and banquets on the sixth floor. The stucco decoration of the banquet hall had motifs of vessels and cups. Musical ensembles played and sang there. From the upper galleries, the Shah watched polo games, military maneuvers, and horse racing in the square below.

This is another site to see. People of all ages visit it, either with a tour guide or by themselves, to admire the tile work and the beauty of this masterpiece.

The Imperial *Bazar* In Isfahan

The *Bazar* of Isfahan is one of the oldest and largest bazaars in the Middle East. Although the present structure dates back to the Safavid era, parts of it are more than a thousand years old. It links the old city with the new.

Niavaran Palace Complex

This is an historical complex in the northern part of Tehran, consisting of several buildings and a museum. The Sahelgraniyeh Palace, built in the 19th century by Nasir al-Din Shah, is inside this complex. The buildings around the palace were demolished by Shah Mohammed Reza Pahlavi. The Niavaran Palace was built by Mohsen Foroughi and completed in 1968. It was the primary residence of the Shah and the Imperial family until the Islamic Revolution because of the climate, the location, and most of all its beauty.

It is amazing to walk through each compound and see the beautiful works of art in each room. The mirror-work and tile-work have been done with such remarkable detail. The palace is open to the public, now, and for a fee you can tour the whole compound (this will take a good half-day). I have taken the tour, myself, and was amazed by the intricate beauty of the art.

Azadi Tower—Freedom Tower

Previously known as the King Memorial Tower, this is the symbol of Tehran, Iran's capital, and marks the entrance to the city. The architect, Hossein Amanat, won a competition to design the monument. Located in Tehran's Azadi Square, it has several fountains around its base and an underground museum. The tower was built with 8,000 blocks of white marble from the Esfahan region, supervised by Iran's master stonemason, Ghaffar Devarpansh Vanosfaderani. It was inaugurated in October 1971.

This masterpiece used to welcome everyone who flew in to Tehran, since it is located in the center of the Tehran airport. Now this has become the domestic airport. Nevertheless, the *Azadi* Tower is still is a very powerful and well-known piece of Iranian architectural design.

Chapter 9

RELIGION

Ancient Iran was all about Islam. Islam—the religion of the Muslims—is a monotheistic faith, regarded as being revealed through Mohammad, as the prophet of Allah (the Arabic word for God.)

In this chapter, I will just give you an overview of this religion, and how it was introduced to people like me. Although I will not go into this topic in depth (not feeling qualified to express any views other than my own), I will try to illustrate as best I can how religion was handed down to us in Iran. Needless to say, other people with much deeper beliefs in Islam have more to say on this topic. [Should you wish to expand your horizons, go to (and explore) http://mto.org/school/index.php?id=22.]

At the age of 30, I did not know much about life as a whole, or why I was a Muslim, other than that it was handed down to me from my parents. Then I had the honor of attending the MTO school of Islamic Sufism and, under the instruction of Hazrat Nader Shah Angha, I started studying. I owe my spiritual master great gratitude for everything that I have learned—not only about Sufism, but also about myself, life, and happiness. He made the integrity and essence of these spiritual teachings available to me; and now I realize for myself why I am a Muslim, beyond the family legacy.

To me, a religion is a guidance, a path that takes you on a spiritual journey. All paths begin and end with God. Having said that, however, I also need to point out that Islam was *the* popular religion in Iran, and those who practiced the Islamic religion did not wish to be around non-Muslims. In the beginning, those who were not Muslim did not practice their religion openly. Jews kept company with Jews, and Christians with Christians. It took a long time until things changed for the better, and people of all religions learned to live in peace with one another.

For as long as I personally can remember, Iran was a country where there was no discrimination based on color or religion. When I was a child, there were Baha'i, Jews, Christians, and people of other religious faiths in Iran. We all learned to live in harmony with one another, even though we each had our own beliefs.

Before my generation, however, there were always people who were prejudiced. I think prejudice comes from the fear of losing what you have, and that you won't be able to have something better. Prejudice comes from people who are rigid and think that what they have is the best and that everyone else is in the dark. Rigidity leaves no room for growth. However, if we keep an open mind we will discover our own most suitable path suitable to God.

If you know that what you will lose will lead to something even better, then you won't be afraid to lose it. What underlies religion is so precious that we cannot really lose anything. With the right attitude, we can only learn more and more about it over time, leading us to practice it with increasing passion.

BASIC RITUALS OF ISLAM

Like any other religion, Islam has various basic rituals. But before going into some of them, I think it's important to say that merely performing these various rituals doesn't make a person a real Muslim. Rituals sometimes can be done in a mechanical way, without deep inner conviction. Religion that's handed down to you doesn't really make you a Muslim—for example, "My

father was a Muslim, so I'm a Muslim." Religion is what you freely choose
for yourself when you're an adult. It's about what you deeply believe in,
what really matters to you.

Bargaining With God (*Nazr Kardan*)

To *Nazr* is very common in our religion, and I am sure in any other beliefs
as well. *Nazer* means that trying to bargain with God for what you want:
"This is what I'm going to do if You do ___ for me." My grandmother used
to say, "*Nazr kardan*, and God will give you what you want." This is the
kind of thing that happens when people seek to have their wishes come
true by donating money to charity, or giving dinners, or anything of that
nature. For instance, they might have a big gathering and feed 100 people
at Ramadan.

Different kinds of *nazer* include: lighting candles; giving food; going
to the tombs of the prophets; or sacrificing a lamb.

However, your relationship with God is not a business deal; it is a
relationship based on love and worship. You don't need to bargain with
God. God will give you what you ask for; you just need to be genuine
when you ask for it, to have a genuine relationship with God. And when
you do the following rituals sincerely, you enter into a genuine relationship
with God.

Namaz Prayer

Namaz is our daily prayer. Every Muslim is supposed to do this prayer
five times a day. *Namaz* means "standing before God, talking to God" (*ro-
be-ghableh*). You need to do *ro-be-ghebleh* when you sit, when you stand,
when you marry, when you die. In all of life, you need to always have a
sense of how close you feel to God, since that is where life begins and ends.

You have to be at least at the age of puberty—at least nine or ten
years old—to start doing *namaz*. People who don't have to do *namaz* are
those who are not yet at puberty, who are mentally unstable, or who are
seriously ill.

Five times a day, you say the same prayer. What varies is how many
times you repeat the sections (a repetition is called a *rakat*).

The prayer is said at these times:

1. <u>In the morning</u>. The morning *namaz* (*sobh*) has two *rakats*, and takes place before sunrise.
2. <u>At noon</u>. The noon *namaz* (*zohr*) has four *rakats*.
3. <u>In the afternoon</u>. The afternoon *namaz* (*bad-az-zohr*) has four *rakats*.
4. <u>Before sunset</u>. Done right before sunset, this *namaz* (*esha*) has three *rakats*.
5. <u>After sunset</u>. This *namaz* (*maghreb*) has four *rakats*.

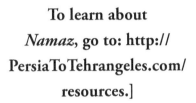

To learn about *Namaz*, go to: http:// PersiaToTehrangeles.com/ resources.]

Washing Before *Namaz (Vazoo)*

An essential purification ritual before starting each *namaz* is *vozoo*—washing your hands and face in order to be pure when you talk to God. The water has to be pure and abundant, not just small trickles or drips, so that you can wash your hands and face completely. The meaning of this ritual is that every time you stand before God, it's important to be pure in every way.

Cleanliness is not only pertaining to the body. It includes morality, as well. *Taher* means "cleanliness inside and out." Islam teaches its followers: Don't gossip. Have a clean vision. Don't look at each other with malice. You have to be *najeeb*—pure. A person who has vicious intent, who rapes, steals, or lusts, is not *najeeb*. Your intentions should be pure and your actions humane, reflecting that purity.

Veiling *(Chador)*

In traditional Islam, women have to wear a veil (*chador*) covering their bodies from their hair all the way down to their toes. The veil should completely cover the hair so that only the round part of the face can be seen (although some *chadors* cover the face, too).

A *mahram* is a person before whom a woman does not have to cover herself, such as her husband, brother, or uncle. *Namahram* is a person before whom the woman does need to cover herself. When men enter a place where women are present, they should always announce their presence by saying, "*Ya Allah*," so the women hear and have time to cover themselves. This custom is meant to guard a woman's purity and respect her privacy.

Consulting A Spiritual Leader For Guidance (*Estekhareh*)

The process of consulting a spiritual leader to receive spiritual guidance about important decisions is called *estekhareh*. This was done more in the old days than now. People would go to a trusted *mullah* or other spiritual leader and ask for guidance and direction in particular matters. Questions might include things like, "I have met this girl and want to marry her. Do you think I should?" Or, "Should I buy this house?" Other questions might concern financial decisions, taking a trip, or whatever was important to the person. The more important it was, the more the person would feel called to consult a spiritual leader.

Then the *mullah* or other spiritual leader would consult his beads, the Qu'ran, or inner divine guidance, and tell the questioner what to do.

Circumcision (*Khatneh Soroon*)

Khateneh soroon—circumcision—was a religious ceremony in Islam, like confirmation in Christianity. It was performed on boys up until six years old. Afterwards, there would be a big party, with the boy present. In the Islamic religion, all males need to be circumcised. Nowadays, thankfully, circumcision is done right away—in the hospital, before the newborn boy is taken home with his parents. Otherwise, could you imagine the scar that circumcising a child of up to six years old would leave?

Women's Religious Gathering (*Rozeh-Moloodi*)

Rozeh-moloodi was a religious gathering just for women, a party that would take place after they had gotten the wish they bargained with God for—a prime example of *Nazer*. However, I always viewed *rozeh-moloodi* as an excuse for the ladies to get together, gossip, and spend some time with their friends, away from their husbands. It was an excuse to get out of the house, because generally women did not leave their homes and party with their friends.

At this gathering, they sang religious songs, played the drum, ate, and prayed. (More gossiping than praying, most likely.)

Fasting During Ramadan (*Rozeh*)

The two most important parts of the Muslim religion are *namaz* (prayers) and *rozeh* (fasting during Ramadan, which lasts for 30 days).

Purpose of the Fast

The purpose of the month of Ramadan is to be wholeheartedly present with God. As with *namaz*, it is expected that everyone will abide by *rozeh* except for people who are mentally or physically incapable, or those who have not yet reached puberty. Women do not have to fast while menstruating.

Timing of the Fast

People fast from sunrise to sunset. Before sunrise, they get up in the morning and eat their main meal, which the woman of the house woke a few hours before sunrise to prepare. After everyone in the family has eaten, each person does *namaz* and then spends the day going within, rather than working in the world. Shops and markets usually are closed for the month, in Iran.

Meaning of the Fast

There's more to fasting than just abstaining from food. The real meaning of the fast is fasting from all the things you're not supposed to do, such as gossip and worldly thoughts. The focus is on the journey within—on internal learning and growth. Much like a tree that is dormant in winter, during *rozeh* you're giving your stomach and brain a rest. (Of course, Muslims who live in the United States have to work, so for them Ramadan is just like any other day.)

Praying During the Fast

In Iran, during the month of Ramadan people usually spend the day at the mosque, where the spiritual leader reads from the Qu'ran and guides his followers to become closer to God. It's a month of spiritual guidance and limited contact with the outer world. But for those who have to work during Ramadan, after they come home and break their fast, they mostly pray during the night to get connected to their spiritual source. Those who have been at the mosque all day come home at sunset (*eftar*), do *namaz*, and then eat the evening meal. Afterwards, they often gather together and pray.

Fasting from Celebration

In the month of Ramadan, there are a few days called *Ahhya*, with no music, weddings, or celebrations. The purpose is to mourn the death of the Prophet Ali, Mohammed's son-in-law who was assassinated in 661. The ceremony lasts from the 19th day of Ramadan—the day Ali was injured (called *Zarbat-khordan*)—until the 21st day, when he died (called *shahadat*). This whole time is called *Ahhya*.

Ending the Fast

After the 30 days, whenever the new moon is sighted by the main spiritual leader, Ramadan is declared to be over, and people are allowed to break their fast. The end of Ramadan usually comes about at different times of night or day, in various countries.

Ceremonial gatherings then follow. People invite others over for *eftar* to break their fast, and the host feeds them. For doing that, he will accrue religious benefit from his generosity (earn a credit toward God called *savab*). This is designed to motivate people to feed others. During Ramadan, it's considered religiously beneficial to feed other people, especially the poor and homeless. One of the main purposes of fasting is learning how it feels to be hungry. This gives you more empathy for those without enough to eat. This is why the two meals eaten daily during Ramadan are supposed to be small and simple.

Donating Money (*Fatriyeh*)

At the end of the month, money (*fatriyeh*) is given away. The amount is supposed to be at least the equivalent of one regular meal for each person in the family. The money is supposed to be donated to a worthy spiritual cause and is meant to ward off evil (in case you didn't properly do your job of inner purification during Ramadan). But even people who feel that their inner focus has been strong enough donate this money. *Fatriyeh* is a way of life, of giving, that they have grown up with. The entire month of Ramadan is also meant to remind those who are fortunate enough to have what they need to be thankful for what they have, and to give to those who do not have enough: to remember the needy, and to appreciate the blessing. Another purpose of giving the equivalent cost of one meal per day is to make it clear how far a dollar would go in helping such people.

Mourning the Death of the Prophet Hussein (*Mo-Harram*)

Mo-Harram takes place in the first month of the Arabic calendar (*sale-ghamari*). This is different from the Iranian calendar, so these events take place at different times each year. *Maharam* is a month of mourning the death of the prophet Hussein, Mohammed's grandson, who was killed in a fight with the prophet Omar and his followers. There are two main events on *Maharam*: one is *Tassoaa*, when Hussein's followers were killed. On the eve of *Tassoaa* was when Hussein called all his followers and told them, "Tomorrow we all will be killed and we will lose the battle, so whoever wants to leave can go now." He ordered them to turn the lights off so no one could see who was leaving. Most of his followers left, but seventy-two stayed. That is why they call it "Hussein and his seventy-two followers." On the day of *Tassoaa*, they lost the battle. All seventy-two of his followers died and he got injured. The other event commemorates the day called *Aashoora*, when Hussein himself died.

Because it is a month of mourning, there is no music. Instead, the Qu'ran is recited, as well as poetry that contemporary poets wrote about the killing of Hussein. This recitation, done in front of a large audience, is called *noheh-khani*. It is done in the form of a gathering called *Sine-zani* and *Zanjir-zani*—the two forms of mourning during these two days. The participants all are men. They start at one side of their community, and as they walk other people join the crowd and end their day at other side of the community, depending who has the *Nazer* of giving them dinner. By this time, the group has grown to hundreds and hundreds of people. This is done from the south to north of the community, for example, or from east to west from the eve of *Tassoaa* to the day of *Aashoora*.

Pilgrimage To Mecca (*Hajj*)

Another important Muslim custom is the *Hajj*, the pilgrimage to Mecca. It's one of the Five Pillars of Islam, along with the profession of faith, prayer, donating money to the poor and the mosque, and fasting during Ramadan.

Every Muslim is required to make this pilgrimage at least once in his or her lifetime, if able to do so. Each year, millions of Muslims travel to *kabeh*, or *khaneh-khoda*—God's house, the most sacred site in Islam. The person who has enough money to pay for this trip, as well as to provide for his family in the meantime, is called *vajebe-o-hajj*. As with prayer and fasting, those who are mentally incompetent, sick, or under the age of puberty aren't allowed to go.

The *hajj* starts in the Arabic month of *zighadeh* and ends at the beginning of the month of *zihajja*. At the *kabeh*, a cuboid-shaped building located inside a mosque, men and women wear white gowns with nothing underneath, symbolizing the day of one's death. The pilgrims circle the *kabeh* seven times in a counter-clockwise direction (*tavaaf*), during a period of several days.

Women must cover their heads. There is no lovemaking; you have to be completely pure and clean. If children have come along, the son stays with the father and the daughter with the mother.

In the old days, it wasn't as easy to go on *hajj* as it is today. There were no cars. You traveled by camel. It could take months to get to Mecca, so if you were willing to undertake this arduous journey you truly met God. Nowadays, you just take a plane, and there are tours that take you to God's house and make all of the arrangements.

When you have completed the pilgrimage, at the end of the last day every person has to sacrifice a lamb (*Eyde-ghorban*: the day of sacrifice). Nowadays, the tour guide takes care of this in advance. As in the Biblical story of Abraham and Isaac, this ceremony is based on God's asking the prophet Ebrahim to sacrifice his son Esmayeel and then relenting and allowing Ebrahim to sacrifice a lamb instead. The person making this sacrifice is supposed to let go of everything impure in himself or herself.

To see a picture of the *Hajj* ceremony, go to: http://PersiaToTehrangeles.com/resources.

Years ago, each sacrificed lamb was just discarded in the desert. But nowadays, the government of Saudi Arabia has built a fine facility for slaughtering, cleaning, and packing the meat and sending it to needy countries. So in this case, advances in technology have resulted in a more humane way of doing things.

When you have successfully gone to God's house and done all the rituals, you are called *hajji* (for males) or *hajjiya* (for females). You are highly respected in the community, and the term *hajji* or *hajjiya* is put before your name as a sign of respect. Or you are called *Hajj Agha*, which means "Mr. *Hajji*."

How Animals Are Killded For Food (*Halal*)

One more religious custom that we have has to do with the way animals are killed. The slaughtering has to be done properly, so that the meat of that animal is considered *halal*. If the animal is not slaughtered properly, its meat is considered *haram*. There are special markets in this country that sell *halal* meat, so that Muslims can buy it there. What you eat is important to who you become; if the animal is not killed humanely, when you eat the meat the anger and fear in its blood have a negative effect on you.

Personally, I do not eat *halal* meat, because I don't believe I can blame what I eat for my behavior. I need to have enough sense and control over myself. We are responsible for every action we take in life. I cannot do something wrong, then say, "I'm a bad person because of all the meat I ate." However, I respect the opinion of those who follow these guidelines. In the same way that I trust the person who sells me meat and tells me that it is *halal*, I feel similarly about organic food: we are charged so much more money for it, and have to take the word of the supplier that it is indeed organic.

COMMENTARY FOR OUR TIMES

As technology becomes more prominent in our lives, we have a tendency to move away from all these customs. In the old days, we were primitive and ignorant; we didn't know how to live right, to enjoy life. As technology advances and countries become more developed, we are learning to do things in a better and more productive way; our skills, our attitudes, our outlook on life are all growing.

When I talk about the old culture, this does not mean that I am promoting the primitive way of life. I am trying to familiarize you with how it was, why it was like that, and how and why things are changing. It's not that they did things wrong in the old days, and today we do it right. But you need to live day by day. Today, you can't live like yesterday. "Day by day" means you value every moment of your life, live it as best you can, and use all the advantages that we have today that we didn't have in the past. For example, the technology used in modern medicine helps us to live healthier, better lives. So I should be able to use all these modern-day advantages to help me become a better person.

Religion is very important, and I truly respect all those who are committed to their beliefs. But I also believe that there should always be room for improvement.

Religion for the New Generation

Now I would like to discuss what religion means to the new generation, so we can have a better understanding of how our children and *their* children feel about the subject.

Religion is an important foundation of a culture, and we need to respect every individual for his or her religious beliefs. After the Iranian migration to other countries, Iranians often married people from another culture or religion. So the question is: how do both people deal with the issue of religion?

In the old Persian culture, both partners had to have the same religion. Jews have had a similar requirement. So the non-Muslim partner had to adopt Islam before being allowed to marry the person they loved.

But today, it's a more relaxed environment, so people who marry often keep their own religion. If one partner in a couple has no particular religious beliefs, sometimes that person finds it easy to adopt their Muslim partner's religion.

This brings up the questions of what the children's religion will be—the father's or the mother's. That is why, for the sake of the children, people with strong religious beliefs often demand that their partner adopt their religion.

If this is your situation, do not treat this matter casually. Make sure that you talk it over with your partner, and decide in advance what the family religion is going to be. You may get deeply involved with someone and fall in love, and only then find out that you need to adopt another religion. I recommend talking it over and finding out before it is too late.

If you have decided to ask your partner to adopt your religion, talk it over and give him or her time to decide. Take them to your religious gathering, but let them come to the decision on their own—and then respect whatever they decide to do. Let them know about your feelings, so they can share theirs with you.

And if you are the parent, do not force your children to follow in your footsteps and adopt your religion. Let them decide for themselves, as religious belief has to come from the heart and be experienced personally. Give them the pros and cons, and let them decide on their own. If you interfere too much, it may affect your relationship with your future son- or daughter-in-law. Do not let skin color or religious beliefs get in the way of the love of your child and his or her partner for each other.

Deciding on Your Religion for Yourself

I'd like to return to a subject that I referred to earlier. Religion that is handed down is not truly a religion. Each individual person has to experience it for himself or herself. When you ask me, "Why are you a Muslim?" my answer is not that it's because my parents were Muslims. The proper answer is that I want to be a Muslim because of what it stands for. So every person has to answer in their own heart which circle they belong to.

Personally, I find all religions to be the same: they teach you the same thing, but they have different ways of getting there. Our destination is God. I always say, "There is only one leader—God—and the rest of us are all followers."

Nowadays, everything is about connection. On the Internet, it's based on how many fans do you have on You Tube, on Facebook. Well, we are all God's fans, and we all want to do things to deserve His kindness and generosity. Muslims often say that Mohammed was the last prophet, with the latest news from God. But I feel no religion is better than any other.

Celebrating Life as a Spiritual Journey

To me, life is a spiritual journey. Everything that I do—every day and moment—has to do with my spirit. When I become tender or loving, that's my spiritual side emerging. And that's how we should all be. By doing this, we would be at peace. Peace starts at home. Then you're at peace with yourself and your family, and in your community and the larger society, as well. It's like a wave. When you drop a drop of water into a bowl, you see how it starts going to the edge of the bowl, getting bigger and bigger.

Religion is a way of life. It will bring us all to a common ground, in which God is the creator and all is well. We need to learn that if we need love, we have to become love; if we want peace we have to become peace. Religion will help us find love and peace. It all starts with one drop—or a smile. Then everything comes after the smile.

That's how we should treat our life: celebrating it every day. It makes life easier. We all have a lot of challenges to deal with every day, but instead of letting that bring anger into your heart, try to multiply love and kindness like that drop of water, and hope that will resolve all the problems. Whenever you are kind and giving, you rise above myself and feel very fulfilled. And every time you hurt someone, that can bring you down so much that you actually have trouble living with yourself.

So every day and every moment, try to get to that height. It feels better! When you're at the height of your being, you're in heaven; when you're at the bottom, you're in hell. So do you want to be in hell all day, or do you want to be in heaven? It takes a lot to be in heaven, but if you keep doing it, it becomes a habit; it becomes part of you. Try to have love take over so that you will *become* love, instead of trying to fight for it or to find it. It *is* you. It's every one of us.

We have to have a destination. What is *your* destination in life? If it's to bring about happiness and make a difference, that's what you should do. If my destination is the "happy house," I'm not going to take a bus that goes to the "anger house." Nor do I want to be around people who drain my energy because of their anger.

Every time I talk about love, it's not just talk. I feel it. It gives me energy. The problems are still there—tell me one person who has no problems! But what's important is how we handle our problems. If you want to let your problems lead you, then you will be in hell. If you handle your problems well, then you can be in heaven.

I hear so many people say, "I want to go where life takes me." *I* don't want to go where life takes me; I want to take life where *I* want to go. That's the journey. Otherwise, it's like getting on a bus that has no destination. You don't know where it's going, or where to get off.

So you have to know where you want to go, what makes you happy. Not being aware is not knowing what you want in life. Every day, I see so many unhappy people. They say they're living life, but to me they're just living a lifeless life, one that has no meaning. They look at me and say, "The reason you're happy is because you have everything you want." I tell them, "You don't even *know* what I want. You don't know what I have and don't have." The reason I'm happy is because I'm contented with what I have, no matter what it is. I don't feel that someone who has a diamond ring on their finger is happier than me.

It all depends on what you want in your life. Try to picture yourself with everything that you want—all the wealth in the world, all the happiness. Yet be honest: will this truly make you content? The more you have, the more you want. This is how humans are; we are never satisfied.

So what you need to learn is that happiness is not about what you *have*. It is all about who you *are*.

WINDOWS TO
HAPPINESS

Throughout this book I have tried to point out ways for you to reach happiness. Here, as we wind down to a close, I would like to give you a summary so you can review it and refresh your thoughts once in a while. Remember: happiness is not something that is given—it is a state of mind. It is entirely up to you to master it, and nobody else.

Give Thanks

Don't get so entangled in the details of daily life that you forget to thank God for all the things you have at your fingertips. It's so easy to be forgetful and not appreciate all the blessings you have.

Be Respectful

If you respect the world you live in today, your grandchildren will live in a better world tomorrow. Respect the environment you live in: you are part of it, and it is what you leave for those who come after you. The more you respect yourself, the more you naturally will want to respect those around you. Also respect the seeds that you plant with your thoughts—the "trees" you grow—so that you can have a crop you will be glad to harvest.

Use Your Life-Energy Well

Instead of complaining about the things you don't have, look around and appreciate what you *do* have. The time you spend complaining is time you lose and will never get back. I call this wasted time "dead time." Take a moment and look at the big picture, so you can realize how small these problems are, compared to how large you are, yourself. Don't waste your energy on something that will not generate more energy for you. Remember ROI—return on investment (from Accounting 101). Always make sure that all your investments in life have a good rate of return.

Let Your Problems Go

Don't hold onto your problems. Instead, let them go. Embrace each moment of your life—that will make it richer. Problems are always part of life. It's how you *look* at them that affects your happiness. Sure, you can focus on your problems, saying, "I don't have time," "I can't make it," "This won't work," or "It takes too long." Or you can say, instead, "I *will* make a difference. I *can* reach my goal. I *will* get up." You need to take charge of your life. Don't be passive and let your life pass you by.

Happiness 101

Here are some basic lessons for living your life so you become happy.

1. Be thankful for what you do have, rather than worrying about what you don't have.
2. Appreciate where you are in life, rather than hoping to be somewhere else.
3. Respect the people who are part of your life, rather than complaining about them.
4. Take control of each situation in your life, rather than giving up.
5. Stand tall and be proud of who you are, rather than disrespecting yourself by saying you will never amount to anything.
6. Lead your life so that you are excited about it, rather than feeling apathetic.
7. Demand what is rightfully yours, rather than giving up on it.

8. Be humble, the more you have, rather than showing it off.

9. Do not stay in a relationship that does not nurture you and will not leave you room to grow.

10. Stop blaming others for where you are in life. Sit behind the wheel and drive yourself to your heaven on earth.

11. Nobody will bring you a plate full of happiness. They are all busy trying to fill their *own* plate.

12. Do not live in a negative environment. Energy is a scarce commodity: spend it wisely, and dedicate it to a good cause.

13. Do not dive into something that you don't know anything about. Test the water, first.

14. Carry yourself with dignity, honesty, and grace, rather than letting greed, jealousy, and malice rule your life.

It's Up to You

You always have the choice of how to live your life, and don't let anyone tell you otherwise. Do your best, and don't be discouraged if you lose. Be proud of your accomplishments. Always try to reach your highest potential without being greedy. There is nothing wrong with having a lot; just keep it in moderation, and share it with those who are not as fortunate as you.

And last, always remember: *you don't have to finish what's on your plate. Always share it.*

A POSTSCRIPT
TO THE READER

Now that you have read your book in its entirety, where are you? Are you in the same place now as when you first started reading? (It may help to close your eyes so you can see inside.)

Yes, I did say "*your* book." If I have been successful in carrying out my intention, this book now has become part of you.

I have tried, here, to show you a number of things that I hope are making their way into your mind, your heart, and even your lifestyle. These include:

- What Persian life and culture were like back home (both the treasures worth keeping and the customs worth updating).
- What it was like for Persian émigrés to come here and seek a good life—whether they adapted easily or held tight to their own ways, or landed somewhere in between.
- What Persian food is about, how the Persian philosophy of eating can serve you, and how becoming familiar with all this can create community in your life.

- How my own story of coming "From Persia to Tehrangeles" can help you understand not only me but also other Iranians and Iranian-Americans—especially the ones in your life.
- So many reasons to be proud to be Iranian-American.

In addition, I hope I have given you inspiration for your own life (wherever you have come from, wherever you are going): how much more you can be, how much farther you can see, and how much more you can take in and make use of. I hope I have been able to show you the height you can claim and the vast horizon you can see. Just open your eyes and take the first step.

And now, to help you continue on your journey, I offer the following suggestions:

1. Look deep inside yourself and bring out the one thing you are most proud of. When you find it:
   - Acknowledge it;
   - Give it all the love you have to give; and
   - Watch it grow.
2. Start nurturing your life by giving it everything it deserves—all that you can give it—and then assert, "THIS IS MY LIFE!"
3. Stand tall and declare:
   - "I am my own responsibility and no one else's."
   - "Throughout life, I will make mistakes, I will take wrong turns, and I will fall, at times—but I will get up every time and not let my falls stop me from reaching the height of which I'm capable."
   - "I am proud of who I am. And I look forward to the person I will become."
   - "I welcome the changes that will be part of my life."
4. Now look into your heart, and tell it, "You are my love-bird. You have the right to leave your nest"—your body—"for a bigger love, when that time comes. But remember: I have to love myself before I can follow you."

In conclusion, dear friend, I hope I have been able to convey the love in my heart to you, through this book. Have a productive and happy life. I am rooting for you all the way.

ABOUT THE AUTHOR

Like many Iranians of his era, Kamran Sharareh came to the United States at a young age to better himself by furthering his education. He obtained a Bachelor of Arts in business and marketing, and a Bachelor of Science in business education, followed by a Masters in business administration. However, as this was his first time leaving the old-country nest, it was a very difficult transaction. He had to start from the beginning, learning a new language and adjusting to a new culture.

Feeling very devoted to his native country and culture, after graduating he took his family and went back to Iran, to do his part as an Iranian. Having worked there for two years, he thought he could do better for himself and his country by moving back to the U.S. And so he returned to America with his wife and U.S.-born daughter, as well as a son on the way.

Following the Iranian Revolution in 1979, his parents and his wife's parents also moved from Iran to the U.S.; and everyone's life changed. To help establish harmony between the older-generation Iranians and the younger generation of Iranian-Americans in this country, Kamran took on the role of being the "buffer generation." Although this sometimes could be arduous, it helped him understand the differences between generations and cultures, and the bridges of understanding that can bring about cooperation, peace, and well-being.

As he grew older and found himself with less family responsibility, he chose to give back and follow his dream. A former restaurateur (in the U.S.), he now holds forth as "Chef KShar," hosting cooking and relationship video demonstrations on his website, KShar's Kitchen (http://www.kshar.net/.) He wrote this book to tell about and preserve the best of the old Persian ways, while also making room for us to learn from the contemporary generation of Iranian-Americans. He lives with his wife, Nazaneen, in Pleasanton, California.

GLOSSARY

A

Aashoora: commemorating the day when Hussein, Mohammed's grandson, died.

Abanbar: a cool place under the house where water was stored, prior to indoor plumbing.

Aghd-konan: the traditional Persian wedding ceremony.

Agil: a mixture of nuts and seeds that is served on the last Wednesday before the Persian New Year.

Ahhya: a ceremony to mourn the assassination of the prophet Ali, lasting from the 19th day of Ramadan until the 21st.

Aks: the reflection in the mirror, representing the opposite of what is there (e.g., before the New Year, the reflection of the *sofreh* in the mirror is what has already happened—the past).

Albalo-polo: sour-cherry rice.

Anbari: a pantry-like room where dried foods were stored.

Aroos: "bride" in Farsi.

Ash reshte: a soup with onions, noodles, vegetable, and garlic.

Atar: perfume.

Atari: shops or *bazars* that sell herbs and spices.

Aza: being in mourning.

Azan: a religious prayer broadcast daily at noon and at sunset to remind everyone to pray.

B

Bademjan: eggplant stew.

Baghali-polo: lima beans and rice with dill.

Bale-boran: deal-making, a phase of the traditional Persian wedding in which the elders of both families meet to discuss who would give what and how much.

Ballal: grilled corn.

Band-andazi: an afternoon party for women to gather at the bride's house to do "threading" (removing all the hair from the bride's face and eyebrows).

Bazar: an important marketing institution in Iran, where goods are bought and sold.

Bazazi: fabric stores.

Beh: quince *sharbat* (syrup water).

Behman: the tenth month of the Persian year.

Boteh-foroosh: the person who gathers dried weed for the fire-jumping ceremony (*char-shanbeh-sory)* just before Persian New Year (*Norooz*).

C

Chador: a veil traditionally worn by women that covers their bodies from their hair down to their toes.

Char-shanbeh-sory: a ceremony shortly before Persian New Year that involves jumping over a fire to bring health and well-being to yourself and your children in the New Year.

Chopgh: a long pipe containing tobacco, often smoked at tea houses.

D

Daluk: a person who worked at the bath house, whose job was to bathe and massage the attendees. There was a male *daluk* for men, and a female *daluk* for women.

Dast-b-dast: when the bride's and groom's hands are put into each other's, on the night after the wedding ceremony, by the father of the bride.

Dastgah: a specific modal system in Persian classical music.

Dido-bazdi: families visiting each other just after the Persian New Year for the purpose of forgiving and forgetting.

Dohol: a Persian folk instrument (double-headed drum).

E

Eftar: sunset; and, by association, the meal that is served at dinner time (sunset) in Ramadan. The act of breaking your fast at that time is called *Eftar*.

Espend: a tray of dried herbs and spices set out on the *sofreh* in the traditional Persian wedding ceremony, supposed to protect the bride and groom against witchcraft.

Estekan: a small glass for drinking tea.

Estekhareh: the process of consulting a spiritual leader to find out what decision to make.

Eyde-ghorban: the day of sacrifice on the last day of *hajj*, when a lamb is sacrificed.

Eyad-norooz: means that the Persian New Year is a happy occasion.

Eyada-shoma-mobarak: "Happy New Year!"

F

Fale Hafez: the practice of using the poet Hafez's book, *Divan Hafez*, for fortune-telling.

Farsh: a *bazar* where carpets are bought and sold.

Farvardin: the first month of the Persian new year.

Fatriyeh: money given away at the end of Ramadan.

G

Gardo: fresh walnut.

Gashen-arosi: the traditional Persian wedding ceremony.

Gatherings after someone in the family has been buried, when they take
place:
- *Shabeh savom*: the night before the third day.
- *Shabeh haft:* the night before the seventh day.
- *Shabeh chaleh:* 40 days after the passing.

Ghableh: Kaabeh is God's house, and *Ghableh* is the direction toward
Kaabeh.

Ghahveh-khaneh: tea house.

Ghamsar: a place in Iran known for its rosewater.

Ghary: the praying and the words that are recited when the deceased is in
the grave.

Ghary-khon: the person who does the singing of the prayers in *ghary.*

Ghasabi: butcher shops.

Ghashne sade: the fire festival.

Ghashogh-zani: a ritual that takes place before Persian New Year, similar to
the American Halloween.

Ghormeh-sabzi: vegetable stew.

Gigar del o gholveh: lamb's liver and heart.

Golab: rosewater.

Golab-giri: the season when water is extracted from rose petals.

Gorough: reserving part or all of a bath house for a celebration.

Gushehs: 365 basic melodies found in traditional Persian music.

H

Haft seen: special items that are put on the *sofreh* (special cloth) for *Norooz*
(Persian New Year).

Haji-firoz: the Persian equivalent of Santa Claus, who makes an appearance
shortly before Persian New Year.

Hajj: the pilgrimage to Mecca.

Hajj Agha: "Mr. Hajji," honorific like *hajji* or *hahhiya.*

Hajji (for males) or *hajjiya* (for females): honorific title for those who have
successfully completed the *hajj.*

Halal: the proper way to kill animals for meat. When an animal is killed
the proper way (Islamic way), the meat of that animal is *Halal.*

Hammom zayeman: a baby's first bathing after birth, a celebration done at the public bath house.

Hamoome-arrosi: gathering at the public bath house to bathe before the traditional Persian wedding.

Haram: meat that is not *halal*, where the animal has not been killed in the proper way according to Islamic law.

Havoo: the second wife that the *none-o-painer* (fresh herbs and feta cheese, on the *sofreh*) is supposed to prevent from ever happening, in the traditional Persian wedding ceremony.

Hookah: a pipe, often smoked in tea houses.

J

Jahiziyeh: furniture and other household materials and goods brought into the newly married couple's home.

Jashne-mehregan: the autumn festival.

Jashne-tirgan: the water festival.

K

Kaf-no-dafen: the burial process.

Kaleh pacheh: lamb's head and feet (a breakfast food).

Kaleh pazi: a place gone to for breakfast, similar to a breakfast diner.

Khaabeh, khabeh-khada: God's house, traveled to on *Hajj*.

Khaneh-tekani: the ceremony of moving everything out of the house and cleaning it in preparation for the New Year.

Khaste-gari: a gathering in which women from the prospective bridegroom's family would go to the bride's house and inspect the bride's face and body.

Khatam: Persian marquetry.

Khatam kari: the art of crafting a *khatam*.

Khateneh: circumcision.

Khateneh soroon: the celebration following *khateneh* (circumcision).

Khazineh: a public bath house that was like a big pool, where everyone bathed together. (Compare with the other kind of bath house, *nomreh*.)

Khoreshte: stew.

Khoresht-karafs: celery stew.

Kofan: a seamless white cloth with verses of the Qur'an on it, for wrapping the body of the deceased prior to burial.

Kondor: frankincense, set out on the *sofreh* in the traditional Persian wedding ceremony.

Korsi: a square table with coals underneath for heating the house in winter, around which the family would sit.

L

Lavosh: an Iranian bread.

Lili lili: "Hooray!"

Loung: a piece of fabric that people at the bath house wrapped around themselves, to keep from being naked.

Lubia-polo: green-bean rice.

M

Maharam: the first month of the Arabic calendar, or *sales-ghamari.* Also a month of mourning.

Mahram: a person before whom women don't have to cover themselves with the *chador.*

Mashdi: a person who has journeyed to Mashhad, where the great-great-grandchild of the prophet Ali is buried.

Mashdi hossien: an artisan who sets tiles or mirrors.

Mehr: the seventh month of the Persian year.

Meyet: the person who has died and is being attended to in the burial process.

Moraba: homemade jam.

Mordeh shoor: a man or woman who is responsible for washing and cleaning the body of the recently deceased person, and preparing it to be put in the grave.

Mordeh shoor khoneh: the place where the body of the deceased is washed by the *mordeh shoor.*

Mullah: cleric or spiritual leader.

N

Naan barbari: a thick bread made of flour.

Naan-sangak: a popular bread in Iran.

Naan taffton: a bread made of flour.

Naba tkhoran: the Qur'an.

Namahram: a person before whom women need to cover themselves with the *chador*.

Namaz: prayer said by Muslims five times a day. It means "standing before God, talking to God" (*ro-be-ghableh*)

- *Sabeh:* morning, meaning that *namaz sabeh* is done in the morning.
- *Zohre:* noon, meaning that *namaz zohre* is done at noon.
- *Bade-zohre: afternoon,* meaning that *namaz bade-zohre* is done in the afternoon.
- *Ashag:* before sunset, meaning that *namaz ashag* is done before sunset.
- *Magreb*: after sunset, meaning that *namaz magreb* is done after sunset.

Namaz meyet: a special prayer done before putting the body of a deceased person (*meyet*) into the ground.

Nanvaei: bakeries.

Nazer: how you act when you really want something from God; bargaining with God.

Nejeeb: one who is pure.

Noheh-khani: poetic recitations commemorating the killing of Hussein, Mohammed's grandson.

Nomreh: a public bath house with special rooms containing a shower and all the facilities. (Compare with the other kind of bath house, *kahazineh*.)

None-o-painer: fresh herbs and feta cheese, part of the *sofreh* in the traditional Persian wedding ceremony.

None sangak: bread signifying life and nourishment, part of the *sofreh* in the traditional Persian wedding ceremony.

Norooz: Persian New Year.

P

Pa-tabhti : the ritual of opening the gifts at the Persian wedding ceremony.

R

Rakat: repetition of sections of a prayer (*namaz*).

Rogane-kermanshahi: a very expensive animal fat that only rich people cooked with.

Rozeh: fasting during Ramadan.

Rozeh-moloodi: a religious gathering just for women, after they got the wish they bargained with God for (*Nazer*) during Ramadan.

S

Sabzah: a birth-and-transformation ritual prior to the New Year, in which you sprout wheat or lentils.

Sakanjeban: a vinegar-and-sugar *sharbat* (syrup water).

"Sale digar bache baghal khoneye shohar": what girls and women who wish to be married say on the 13th day of the New Year (*Sizdeh-badar*). It means, "Next year this time, I hope to be married with a child, in my husband's house."

Sale-ghamari: the Arabic calendar year.

Sale-shamsi: the calendar the Iraninan people go by.

Sal-e-tahvil: when the earth passes through the equinox, which announces the Persian New Year (*Norooz*).

Samovar: a metal container that holds water and has a cavity in the middle to hold hot coals. A teapot is placed on top.

Savab: doing something that will result in the good of others.

Setar: an ancient Persian musical instrument.

Shaba yalda: the winter festival.

Shabeh chaleh: a gathering that takes place 40 days after someone in the family has been buried.

Shabeh haft: a gathering that takes place the night before the seventh day after someone in the family has been buried.

Shabeh savom: a gathering that takes place the night before the third day after someone in the family has been buried.

Shahadat: anniversary of the death of the Prophet Mohammed's son-in-law Ali, on the 21st day of Ramadan.

Shahnameh: the epic story of Persia, written by the poet Ferdousi between 977 and 1010 A.D.

Shamas-o-emareh: a famous *bazar* in Iran.

Sharbat: syrup water.

Shirin-polo: a rice dish made with saffron, orange peel, carrot, sugar, and barberry—often served at Persian weddings.

Sine-zani: one of two forms of mourning done during *Maharam*.

Sizdah-badar: the 13th day of the Persian New Year.

Sofreh: a large ceremonial tapestry.

Sofreh-aghd: a part of the traditional Persian wedding ceremony where the bride and groom would sit next to the *sofreh*, which contained a candelabra and a mirror, among other items.

Sorna-Zorna: a Persian folk instrument.

T

Tahar-e Berelian: the "Hall of Brilliance," an Iranian landmark.

Taharat: cleansing at the public bath house before doing prayers at sunrise for a man and woman who had had sex the night before.

Tahchin: chicken with saffron rice.

Taher: cleanliness inside and out.

Tahir: athletic displays of musicianship in classical Iranian music.

Tajrish: a famous *bazar* in Iran.

Takht-gah: a raised chair at the *zor-khaneh* (house of strength) where only the spiritual leader would sit.

Tanoor: a clay oven.

Tar: an ancient Persian musical instrument.

Tasnif Foroosh: song-sellers.

Tassoaa: one of two events that take place on *Maharam*.

Tauhid: union with the mystical Beloved, as put forth by Rumi.

Tavaaf: the counter-clockwise direction in which pilgrims circle the *kabeh* when on *hajj*.

Tir: the fourth month of the Persian calendar. It means "water," "purity," "lightness."

Torshi: home-made pickled foods.

V

Vajebe-o-hajj: a person who has enough money to make the *hajj* pilgrimage and provide for his family.

Vazoo: washing your hands and face in order to be pure when you talk to God.

Z

Zarbat- khordan: mourning on the day Ali, the prophet Mohammed's son-in-law, was injured (the 19th day of Ramadan).

"Zardi-man-az-to, sarkhi-to-az-man": what people said during the fire-jumping ceremony of *Char-shanbeh-sory* shortly before the New Year. Literally, it means, "You take my yellowness and give me your redness." Symbolically, it means, "Give me happiness and take away my sickness and sorrows."

Zangir-zani: one of two forms of mourning done during *Maharam*.

Zereshk-polo: barberry rice.

Ziloo: carpet and rough-carpet weaving.

Zor-khaneh: a "house of strength"—a club where men went to become strong and show off their strength.

TO LEARN MORE

To find out more about:

- Chef KShar's Kitchen,
- The Persian Cooking Academy,
- Live to Feed (nonprofit organization), and
- All else in this book please visit,

www.kshar.net and **www.PersiaToTehrangeles.com**.

Printed in the USA
CPSIA information can be obtained
at www.ICGtesting.com
JSHW022344140824
68134JS00019B/1683